THE COMPLETE GUIDE TO MALTIPOOS

David Anderson

Cover photo courtesy of Amanda Hazy

TABLE OF CONTENTS

CHAPTER NINE

INTRODUCTION
The perfect dog: sounds like a dream, but is it possible?

It is possible, if you have a Maltipoo. Maltipoos are a crossbreed of Poodles and Maltese. Both Poodles and Maltese are highly esteemed as show dogs and loyal companion dogs but have some defects that make most pet owners wary of them. When bred together, they produce the perfect combination that nobody can resist falling in love with.

Maltipoos are a bundle of perfection, combining the right amount of personality, spunk, cuteness, and energy. Even with all of that personality, they love a good cuddle on your lap. Maltipoos are considered to be an ideal companion dog.

In this book, you will learn how you can work with your Maltipoo's moldable personality and teach it to be a well-behaved angel. You will learn how to create the perfect environment to teach your Maltipoo and how to avoid creating bad habits that will come back to haunt you later on in life.

The day you decide to bring your new Maltipoo puppy home, you make a promise to care for its every need. That can seem to be a big responsibility. With the suggestions found in this book, taking care of your Maltipoo will be a breeze. You will learn how to groom, feed and exercise your adorable little Maltipoo.

Common behavior issues are discussed in this book, providing troubleshooting and strategies on how to fix bad habits or behavior. There is a whole chapter dedicated to one of the most challenging aspects of obedience training: potty training. It will make that phase of your Maltipoo's life (and yours) a simple and easy one, as the suggestions found in that chapter will have the most stubborn of dogs potty trained in no time.

You will also learn the essentials of proper nutrition for your Maltipoo and how to choose the best dog food for your Maltipoo.

Having a Maltipoo puppy can be one of life's most rewarding experiences. Dogs can relieve people's stress, improve our health and remind us that true love does exist. You will find raising your Maltipoo puppy to be one of the richest and most satisfying chapters of your life.

This book will become your go-to guide throughout your Maltipoo's life, with helpful hints and reminders that will prove to be practical far into your Maltipoo's adulthood.

Can you raise the perfect Maltipoo puppy? Absolutely! Your little bundle of joy will be the proof that a perfect dog does exist. It just requires some patience and love on your part to apply the helpful suggestions found in this book.

CHAPTER ONE
What is a Maltipoo?

Wouldn't it be great if puppies could stay puppies? Everyone loves puppies, with their adorable puppy appearance and cute puppy behavior, but it lasts such a short time. They grow up into dogs in a matter of months, losing that puppy charm.

Is there a dog that stays like a puppy far into its teen years?

Yes there is, and it is called a Maltipoo. One of the reasons that it has become so popular in the past few years is because it maintains its puppy-like appearance and behavior. With a Maltipoo puppy, you can have a puppy that never grows old.

But what exactly is a Maltipoo?

Standard Poodle

Is it a Poodle or a Maltese?

The Maltipoo isn't really a breed, but a crossbreed between two very popular breeds, the Maltese and the Poodle. This crossbreed brings out the best of both.

Crossbreeding a Maltese and a Poodle produces a friendly and outgoing dog that is also considered to be one of the world's cutest dogs.

Breeders usually breed a purebred Maltese with a Toy Poodle. In some cases they use a Miniature Poodle, which produces slightly larger puppies that are still extremely adorable. Their size makes them ideal for being cuddly lapdogs.

So what exactly is a crossbreed?

Dogs that have been crossbred are often called "designer dogs". A crossbred dog is the result of breeding one purebred dog to a different kind of purebred dog. In the case of the Maltipoo, it is a mix of the purebred parents the Poodle and the Maltese.

The sole intention of crossbreeding is to create puppies that share the personality traits of both parents. For the last thousand years, breeders have been mixing different breeds to achieve a certain appearance, temperament or ability. This is the case with the Maltipoo.

Crossbreeding dogs has become very popular in the past decades, due to the belief that crossbreeds will be healthier and stronger than the dogs in their purebred lineage. Correctly choosing the lineage for crossbreeding can result in a puppy worth more than its purebred parents.

Depending on breeding, a typical Maltipoo will be around four to seven pounds and stand about ten inches. If one parent was a Miniature Poodle, which is a little larger than the Toy Poodle, the Maltipoo will be a little bigger, being around five to fifteen pounds and standing up to fourteen inches. The size and weight of the Maltipoo depends on the type of Poodle used in breeding.

Maltipoo colors

Maltipoos can either have a scruffy or curly coat that normally is white and cream colored but sometimes can be other colors.

It is common for a Maltipoo to be born a certain color, be a different color at sixteen weeks, and when fully-grown have a completely new coat color. This is normal because the Maltipoo has both Poodle and Maltese genes and this fading effect is very common with Poodles. If the Maltipoo's color does not change, it is called "holding," but if it changes, it is called "fading." With some Maltipoo pups, their coat may fade; others darken, and others might not change at all.

The ever so popular apricot color Maltipoo will have an almost peachy apricot color for the first year, but as it grows, its coat becomes more of a light creamy peach color.

Some Maltipoo pups' coat colors will change according to the season. For example, a black Maltipoo will have a deep black color during the winter months, but during the summer months its coat fades to a charcoal color.

Your Maltipoo will be full of wonderful little surprises, one of which is seeing its coat change as it turns into a playful adult. The changes happen because of the strong Poodle genes your Maltipoo has.

Maltese

Deciding which Maltipoo color you think is the cutest will be up to you!

Here is a list of Maltipoo colors and their description:

White Maltipoo: This is considered to be one of the most traditional colors for a Maltipoo. Purebred Maltese are as white as snow and if bred with a pure white poodle (no color genes for the past 5 generations), the puppies will be white.

Red Maltipoo: This color is extremely rare for a Maltipoo because the genes are 50/50. The Maltese will need to be bred with a red Poodle.

Cafe Au Lait Maltipoo: A beautiful light brown color resembling milk chocolate or cafe au lait. It can also be referred to as a tan, brown, golden or bronze colored dog.

Black and white Maltipoo: These Maltipoo pups will have white and black markings on their faces, chests, tummies and paws.

Black Maltipoo: A black Maltipoo is extremely rare, as one of the parents is always snow-white. A true black Maltipoo will have a solid black color with no other markings. A true black coat will not change color.

Apricot Maltipoo: The coat can be the creamiest apricot color to a solid apricot color. Some Maltipoo pups look as if they have put apricot or reddish highlights in their hair.

Gray Maltipoo: If a Maltipoo is born gray, it will stay gray for life.

Silver Maltipoo: Sliver is a diluted grey color with a very shiny coat. The Maltipoo will be born with a very dark black/grayish coat that will fade to a silver color.

Silver Beige Maltipoo: The puppy will be born brown and the color will change at around six to eight weeks to a silver beige color.

Cream Maltipoo: This color appears to be a stark white, until it is placed near a white Maltese; then it can be seen that it is an off-white, almost champagne color.

Bronze Maltipoo: A shiny, lighter brown color that is almost tan.

Blue Maltipoo: This is a very rare color for a Maltipoo. It appears to be pure black until placed in direct sunlight and then the blue color will shimmer from the coat.

Brown Maltipoo: A deep brown color like a Hershey's chocolate bar.

Maltipoos come in a wide variety of colors depending on their parents' genes and backgrounds. The hard part will be deciding what color to pick.

Different coat types

There are three different types of coats for Maltipoos. The type of coat your Maltipoo has will indicate whether the Poodle or Maltese genes are more dominant. Here is a brief description of the different types of coats your Maltipoo could have.

Straight and silky: If a Maltipoo has a straight and silky hair, the Maltese gene is dominant. Normally, this type of coat will have a lighter color. It will tangle easily.

This type of coat allows for many grooming options: it can be left to grow long, as with a Maltese, or cut short for the puppy cut.

Thick and curly: Poodles have curly hair, so the dominant gene is from the poodle. The texture will be a little denser than the straight coat and more likely to mat up and tangle.

Tangles should be dealt with promptly, as a little tangle can lead to a big mess in no time. It is recommended to groom this type of Maltipoo every three weeks.

Wavy and wiry: This type of coat is a sign of bad breeding. Stay far away from a Maltipoo puppy with this type of easily tangled, high-maintenance coat.

Facts sheet about Maltipoo Dogs

Pronunciation	Mault-eh-Poo
Common nicknames	Moodle, Malt-A-Poo, Maltepoo, Multi-poo, Maltese-Poodle, Maltipoodle
Breed history	Cross between a purebred Toy Poodle and a purebred Maltese
Average weight	5 to 12 pounds
Average height	8 to 14 inches
Life expectancy	15 years
Maturity	1 year old considered an adult
Average litter size	4 to 6 puppies
Shedding	Very light shedders
Purpose	Companion, lap dogs

Maltipoo personality traits

Personality lies in the genes. Nature is responsible for creating all living creatures' personalities. This is especially true with humans. Of course, how our personality is nurtured will have an effect on who we will become as adults.

How often have we observed a little boy with his father, and used the expression "like father, like son"? This ancient English proverb means that the son's behavior, conduct, and features resemble that of his father. It is because of the boy's genes, which make him a smaller version of his father.

With dogs, it is very similar. Their personality traits depend upon genes that they inherit from their parents. For this reason, before we can understand the personality traits of the Maltipoo, we need to know about the pros and cons of its parents, the purebred Maltese and the Poodle.

Maltese

Some of the pros with Maltese are that they don't require too much exercise and can be easily entertained with simple games and toys, such as "get the ball out from under the cabinet." They are very playful and are generally happy to play alone. The Maltese isn't a heavy shedder even though it has a beautiful coat of hair. They are also very easy to train.

A few cons with Maltese puppies are that they are extremely difficult to potty train. Also, because of their size, they are very fragile. Because of this, they are not recommended for families with small children or bigger dogs that might decide they would make a good afternoon snack. They are high-maintenance with grooming and also suffer from chronic allergies and itchy skin.

Maltese Puppies

13

Poodle

Some of the pros with Poodles are that they are hypoallergenic, which makes them the ideal pet for those who suffer from allergies. They don't shed, so it is quick and easy to clean up after them. Poodles are considered to be excellent watchdogs. They are also extremely intelligent, making them very easy to train.

A few of the cons with Poodles actually come from their high intelligence. Because they are so intelligent, they have the tendency to get bored rather quickly and become irritable. If they are not occupied constantly, they will find something to do that might not be very pleasing to the owner, such as destroying your leather couch. They need a large area that allows them to get plenty of exercise, so having a large yard is required. If not properly trained, Poodles will become very high-strung and disobedient.

The combined pros of these two breeds make them the ideal parents to make a perfect little Maltipoo puppy that will bring you years of happiness. But what will your Maltipoo puppy be like? Let's consider some of its personality traits in the following list.

Playful and outgoing

Maltipoo puppies love everyone, whether it be humans or other dogs, and they love companionship. A Maltipoo puppy's only desire in life is to please its owners and it will have you smiling and laughing within

Standard Poodle

minutes. But, because they love everyone and everything so much, they are not the best choice for a watchdog.

Since they have such a good-natured temperament, they can be ideal for pet owners who have other pets in the house already. Caution is needed, however, because of their size and fragility. Small children and bigger dogs could hurt a little Maltipoo without even trying.

Intelligent

Maltipoos are considered to be one of the world's cutest dogs. But don't let those beautiful brown eyes fool you. Behind the cuteness is a head full of intelligence, inherited from its purebred Poodle parent.

Their high intelligence makes potty training and other training a breeze. But because of their intelligence, they do have a need to be mentally stimulated. Like their purebred Poodle parents, they have a tendency to suffer from separation anxiety; but with loving discipline they can be trained to behave when left alone.

Energetic

Maltipoos make ideal pets for small apartments or houses with small yards because they are so tiny they don't need too much space to run around. They do, however, thrive on regular walks around the block or to the park.

Regular walks help keep your Maltipoo mentally and physically stimulated. One of the outstanding qualities of Maltipoos is that they maintain their puppy personality well into adulthood. That means they will have tons of energy that will need to be burned off. Regular short walks will get rid of this excess energy and prevent misbehaviors like barking, whining and chewing your furniture.

Each individual Maltipoo's energy level will depend on which parent's genes are dominant. Dominant Poodle genes will result in a more hyperactive pup, but dominant Maltese genes will result in a more laid-back pup.

Other personality traits

Maltipoos are very loyal to their owners and love to spend time with their human parents.

They are inside dogs and cannot tolerate outdoor temperatures for very long. If you have a Maltipoo, be prepared for it to live with you inside of your house and be taken outside only for bathroom needs, walks, playtime and exercise. Maltipoos will not survive if left outside for long periods of time.

As we can see, the Maltipoo crossbreed produces a very affectionate and playful puppy, resulting in an ideal companion dog.

Maltipoo history

❝ *Maltipoos are the sweetest, most loving, smartest puppy you could ever find. They love everyone and socialize well with people and other pets."*

Dena Fidanza
denasdoggies.com

The history of Maltipoos begins in the United States. They were created to be small, faithful and loving companions. Breeding a Maltese and a Poodle, creating a Maltipoo, has become increasingly popular in the past 10 to 20 years.

The Maltipoo was specifically created to be suitable for people with allergies. It has been said that the Maltipoo is hypoallergenic because of its coat. There is no proof, however, that this statement is true. All dogs produce dander and saliva that carry allergens that may cause allergic reactions in certain people.

The poodle's history appears to have begun in Germany, where it was bred to be a water retriever for hunting duck and other fowl. Poodles come in all sorts of colors and three sizes: standard (the original), miniature and toy. The breed finally standardized in France. They have been highly esteemed from the 1400s up until our day because of their intelligence.

The Maltese dog's history goes back to about 500 B.C. This breed was recorded on a Greek amphora. The breed's name and origins are believed to have come from the Mediterranean Island of Malta. History suggests that it was bred to help control rodents, but soon became popular among the noble women. Maltese dogs have been highly esteemed as a ladies' dog throughout the ages up until our day.

As we can see, the lineage of the Maltipoo is very rich and full of history. Both the Poodle and the Maltese were highly regarded throughout history for their personality traits and beautiful appearance.

Your own little Maltipoo puppy will become part of your personal family history by quickly becoming a beloved member of your family.

Interesting facts about Maltipoo puppies

- It is common to see Maltipoo puppies with tearstains around their eyes but crying from feeling sad does not cause it. It can be caused from a number of things, such as dry eyes, an allergen in their food, or food dye. Observing environmental factors and giving them a healthy wholesome diet with no artificial colors can eventually eliminate the tearstains.
- Poodles have a curly coat of hair and Maltese have beautiful long straight hair. Because the Maltipoo is a crossbreed, the parents' genes will come into play when determining what type of hair your Maltipoo will have. It could be curly or straight. Both Poodles and Maltese need regular grooming sessions to prevent their hair from becoming matted and tangled, so expect the Maltipoo to, as well. Maltipoos love baths and it actually provides an important health benefit for them as it prevents their skin from drying out and becoming itchy. It is recommended to bathe your Maltipoo every three weeks. If your Maltipoo has curly hair, it will need to be professionally groomed about every four to six weeks.
- There are two different ways to spell this crossbreed's name. The American Canine Hybrid Club and the Designer Dogs Kennel Club have it registered as Malt-A-Poo. The International Designer Canine Registry spells it Maltipoo. The latter is the most widely recognized way to spell Maltipoo.
- Maltipoos have first and second generations, first generation being the result of breeding a purebred poodle and a purebred Maltese, and second generation being the result of breeding two Maltipoo dogs.
- Small dogs normally have longer life spans than larger dogs.
- They do not make good watchdogs because of their size and their friendly personality.
- Full-grown Maltipoos can easily fit into a large bag and be carried with you everywhere.
- Maltipoo dogs have a sweet and gentle personality, so they make great therapy dogs.

In summary, a Maltipoo is a cross between a Poodle and a Maltese; they are considered to be designer dogs because the cross brings out the best in both breeds. Poodles and Maltese are considered to be breeds that don't shed, therefore many people consider the Maltipoo to be a hypoallergenic dog.

They are very intelligent dogs that love to socialize and be around people. They are considered to be the eternal puppy, keeping their puppy-like appearance and behavior far into adulthood.

CHAPTER TWO
Is a Maltipoo puppy for you?

It has been said that a dog is man's best friend. But why is that? Having a dog can be one of life's most rewarding experiences. Dogs provide long lasting companionship and unconditional love. Plus, studies have proven that having a dog can bring many health benefits, such as lowering blood pressure, warding off depression and reducing stress.

Also, having a dog is the best way to guarantee you will get out for your daily walks because your four-pawed best friend will need to exercise too. A dog is a great motivational tool to get you off your couch and out for a nice brisk walk.

Dogs have the capability to make the world's grumpiest person break down and smile in a matter of seconds. They make us feel loved and cared for and are always ready to happily greet us when we walk through the front door.

Choosing which type of puppy to bring home to become your new best friend can be a very daunting experience. With so many different types of dogs, how can you know if a Maltipoo puppy is right for you?

The ideal family for a Maltipoo

" *Maltipoos are very 'clownish'. They seem to have a special 'happy dance' that, once acknowledged, gets repeated frequently.* **"**
Terry Schulte
valleypuppypaws.com

The fact that you are considering getting a Maltipoo means that you are looking for a small dog. Let's consider the ideal family for a Maltipoo to see if your family lifestyle is a good fit for a Maltipoo.

Living environment
Maltipoos are very sensitive to the cold and harsh environment outside of your home. They cannot survive being outside for long periods. They are lap dogs and are smaller than some cats. They require a warm, cozy living environment.

Photo Courtesy of
Mary Papadopoulos

Also, considering their size, they have almost no means for defending themselves against larger dogs or birds of prey. Being left outside alone for a long period can cause your Maltipoo to feel anxious and stressed.

They need to spend the majority of their day inside your house, where it is warm and safe. Maltipoos cannot tolerate hot and cold weather. In the cold winter months, you might need to get a little sweater for your Maltipoo to prevent it from getting sick when going outside for walks and potty breaks.

✔ If you plan on having your dog live indoors with you and be part of your family, then a Maltipoo is the dog for you.

Maltipoos can make ideal pets for those who live in an apartment building or have a very small yard. They don't need too much space to burn off their excess energy. The best way to burn off your Maltipoo's energy is to take it for short walks around the block.

✔ If you live in an apartment building or have a small yard, then a Maltipoo is the dog for you.

Maintenance

The Maltipoo has inherited a beautiful coat from its parents, the Maltese and the Poodle. It can either be curly or have a nice shaggy coat, but it can easily become matted and knotted, causing discomfort, itchy skin, and clumps of hair that will drop off around your house. How can you prevent that from happening?

Daily brushing is the key to preventing the coat from forming unsightly knots and hairballs. Poodles, Maltese and Maltipoo dogs don't shed their hair, which makes them ideal for allergy sufferers.

Maltipoos are considered to be high maintenance because you have to brush them daily, but really, compared to the time you could spend vacuuming dog hair off your carpet and furniture, spending less than five minutes a day grooming your dog is a breeze.

✔ If you have five minutes a day to pamper your dog by brushing it and dislike finding dog hair all over your house, then a Maltipoo is the dog for you.

Also, if you happen to have a curly-haired Maltipoo, it will need to be professionally groomed every five to six weeks. As with most indoor dogs, it is highly recommended to bathe your pup every three weeks, to prevent itchy, dry skin.

New dog owners

For new dog owners, it can feel very intimidating to bring home a little puppy, especially when it has to do with potty training. Maltipoo pups are very intelligent and are fast learners.

They respond well to firm but loving discipline. Training doesn't require too much time or effort. You need to show your little Maltipoo that you are the "head of the pack" or the boss. Normally, a firm "No" is all it takes to get the message through. Maltipoo pups are eager to please their owners and are not as stubborn as other small dogs.

✔ If this is your first puppy and you are nervous about training, then a Maltipoo puppy is for you, as it is an easy dog to train.

Be cautious about spoiling it as a puppy, as it will turn into a disobedient 'bratty' dog when it gets older.

Small children and large dogs

If you have small children or grandchildren that often come over to your house, it is not recommended to have a Maltipoo. No matter how many times you tell little ones not to handle or pick up your little puppy, they will not be able to resist the temptation. Little ones can accidently drop or squeeze your little Maltipoo puppy too hard and fracture a bone or cause other damage.

✔ If you have little children over to your house often, it isn't recommended to get a Maltipoo puppy.

If you have larger dogs, they have the tendency to play rough with the smaller dog. Chances are your little Maltipoo will suffer dire consequences. If you have older dogs, they might be suitable to be around your Maltipoo because they aren't as rambunctious as younger dogs.

✔ If you have larger dogs that are hyperactive, it isn't recommended to get a Maltipoo puppy.

If your large hyperactive dogs are outside dogs and the time spent with your baby Maltipoo outside will be supervised, it may be safe to consider getting a Maltipoo.

Separation Anxiety

Maltipoos bond very quickly and closely to their owners and when the owners are not around, they quickly become concerned, worried and even go into panic mode. Separation anxiety can turn the most laid back dog into a destructive monster, chewing on anything that is in front of it, barking, whining and creating chaos throughout the house.

Maltipoos thrive in environments where there is someone home during the day or if you can take your dog to work with you. Maltipoo puppies are extremely social and just love being around people. If your work schedule takes you out of your house frequently and for long hours throughout the day, it might be wise to consider another type of dog that fits in better with your lifestyle.

✔ If you are planning on leaving your dog alone frequently, it isn't recommended to get a Maltipoo puppy.

If you decide to get a Maltipoo, you must realize that it will not be happy living in the laundry room; it will need to have free run of the house. If it can see you or other family members but can't get to you, it will show its displeasure by whining and barking constantly and may panic.

Where should you buy your Maltipoo?

"Questionable breeder," "Puppy Mill," "Next Day Pets": these are common expressions used in the puppy world today. How can you be sure that you are buying your Maltipoo puppy from a reputable breeder?

Good breeders are more interested in finding the right family for their puppies than they are in the money. When talking to a breeder, pay attention to whether they are open about the parents' past and health. They should ask questions about you and what kind of life you can give their puppy. A good breeder is open and honest; they will show you by their conversation that they genuinely care about the future of their puppies.

- Avoid breeders that are only concerned about how soon you can take the puppy away and if your credit card or PayPal went through.
- Ask your veterinarian about reputable breeders in the area.
- Avoid websites that advertise "multiple litters available immediately" or "puppies always available." Quick purchases are very convenient but almost are never from a reputable breeder.
- Remember: the best things in life take time. It will take time to find the right breeder for your Maltipoo puppy and then you might have to wait until there is a litter.
- Look for a breeder that doesn't breed their dogs until they are over two or three years old.
- Say no to a puppy whose parents are unfriendly and won't let you approach them or growl at you, or if any of the puppies do any of those things. Bad behavior is learned from the parents.

*Photo Courtesy of
Sue Watson*

It is advisable to put as much effort into researching where to buy a puppy as you would into buying a vehicle or an appliance.

Before you buy a Maltipoo, it is important to research the health of both the parents. If possible, make sure both parents have a health clearance from the Orthopedic Foundation for Animals for the thyroid and knees (patella). Also ask to see certification from the Canine Registry Foundation that the eyes are normal, and if possible request to see their DNA test for progressive retinal atrophy.

These health problems won't manifest themselves until the Poodle or Maltese reaches full maturity, so health clearances are not given if the dog is younger than two years old.

Just remember, a Maltipoo will reflect the personality of its parents. An irresponsible breeder can make a mess of the combined genetic problems from unsuitable parents. This can create a whiny, noisy little tyrant of a dog that would be almost impossible to train, with a potentially long, expensive list of health problems.

What about adopting a Maltipoo from a shelter?

Sadly, many Maltipoos end up in shelters or have been rescued from families that weren't caring for them properly. These dogs are in dire need of someone to love and care for them.

But how can you go about looking for a rescued Maltipoo?

Use the internet to search for a Maltipoo in your area. There are many websites that can help narrow your search to a general area, or to specific traits you are looking for (such as dogs that have been previously housetrained). Many animal shelters have websites that can direct you to rescue groups in your area.

When adopting a Maltipoo puppy or dog, here is a list of questions that you can ask before you fall in love with your puppy:
1. Does it socialize well with other animals?
2. How does it respond to shelter workers, children, visitors, etc.?
3. What is its age?
4. Is it potty trained?
5. Has it ever bitten anyone (that they know of)?
6. Does it have any health issues?

Wherever you end up acquiring your Maltipoo, make sure you have a contract with the seller, shelter or rescue group that clearly explains the responsibilities for both parties.

As soon as you adopt your Maltipoo, or purchase it from a reputable breeder, take it immediately to your veterinarian for a checkup. A good veterinarian will often be able to spot any future concerns or health problems. Also, you can set up a regimen to keep your puppy in good health for years to come.

Pros and cons of having a Maltipoo

66 *Maltipoos are great for condos, apartments or a home with a small yard. They can meet their exercise requirements while playing games or fetch indoors."*

Rebecca Posten

riversidepuppies.biz

Everything in life has pros and cons. In many situations, the cons unfortunately outweigh the pros. But this isn't the case with a Maltipoo puppy; the pros definitely outweigh the cons. This is why the Maltipoo is quickly becoming one of the America's most popular dogs.

Pros

- Maltipoos are extremely intelligent, so they are very easy to house-train. They also respond well to litter box training for those that live in high-rise apartment buildings.
- They are wonderful dogs for first time puppy owners because of their desire to please their owners. They are quick learners and respond to love.
- Maltipoo pups are ideal for living in small spaces such as apartments, as they are easily satisfied with a frequent walk around the block. Having a Maltipoo is also a motivational tool to help you start walking more and get more exercise, which benefits your health.
- Maltipoos don't shed, so you will have no need to be constantly cleaning up your house to remove the dog hair. Also, your clothes won't be covered with dog hair every time you decide to pick up your pet.
- Maltipoo dogs are like eternal puppies, keeping their puppy-like appearance and behavior far into adulthood.
- They are very loyal companion dogs that love being with you. With your Maltipoo puppy, you will have found your new best friend.

25

- Maltipoos are very adaptable to changes, as long as you are still there. This makes them ideal travel companions, since they don't get upset by being in new settings and environments.
- Maltipoos love cats and quickly become friends with them. So if you have a cat, don't worry--they will soon be playing non-stop and cuddling together during naptime.

Cons

- Maltipoos are very small and their size makes them fragile and defenseless. Care is needed when handling them. Maltipoo pups are not recommended for families with small children. Young children often play rough and could accidently drop the Maltipoo, causing a fracture.

  Maltipoos love children and children love them. Sadly, children under the age of six years old can easily injure them. For this reason, it is not recommended to have a Maltipoo in a house with small children. If small children frequently come over to your house, teach them how to handle your Maltipoo and never leave them unsupervised with your little puppy.

- They are ill-suited as guard dogs because of their size. They can bark and maybe bite around the ankles but that's about all. Also, their friendly disposition doesn't make them cautious about strangers.
- All dogs, no matter the breed, will have some health problems. It is important to know the potential problems so you can take preparative measures now.
- Maltipoos were crossbred to be hypoallergenic dogs for those who suffer from allergies. But each dog is different in how many allergens it produces. All dogs produce some dander, which is the cause of most allergies.
- Maltipoo pups are considered to be high-maintenance since they need to be brushed daily and bathed every three weeks, to prevent their skin from drying out.

As you can see, the pros outweigh the cons--and the cons are not deal breakers. Deciding to have a Maltipoo puppy will be one of the best decisions of your life. It will quickly become your best friend and faithful companion.

But how will your Maltipoo puppy get along with rest of your four-pawed family members?

Maltipoos and other dogs

Maltipoos are very social dogs and generally get along with other dogs and pets, whether they have been raised with them or not.

There is always some form of sibling rivalry in any family, but the rivalry can be controlled when the parents step in and put a stop to it before it gets out of hand. Expect some sibling rivalry in the beginning when you bring your Maltipoo home.

Vaccines and other dogs

Puppies are normally vaccinated when they are four months old. It is recommended to avoid socializing a young puppy with other dogs, since you can't know with certainty if they have been vaccinated and are safe for your new puppy.

Is it safe to introduce my puppy to my older dog?

If your adult dog is up to date on its vaccinations, introducing an infection to either dog is very unlikely. If you have an unvaccinated dog that is already sick, it could be very dangerous for your puppy.

Ideal habitat for a Maltipoo

" *If you are the athletic type that likes hiking, jogging, and playing at the park; or if you like staying indoors watching TV, Maltipoos can be a great companion to you in both environments."*

Spencer Carranza

maltipoored.com

For as long as human history goes back, there are records of dogs being companions for humans. Most dog breeds that exist today cannot survive without human companionship. They are unable to live in the wild or on the streets without someone caring for and nurturing them.

Dogs are happiest with human companionship, and honestly, humans are happier with canine companionship. Since dogs are domesticated animals, they need to live in protected habitats with shelter, warmth, food and love. Most dogs are unable to find food on their own.

What is the ideal habitat for your Maltipoo?

Companionship

As we have learned, Maltipoos are very social and quickly form a tight bond with their owners. They love to make their owners happy. When you bring your Maltipoo home, it will become very attached to you.

Your Maltipoo will be the most faithful and loyal dog you will ever have. All you have to do to gain its friendship is to show it love and attention.

Dogs adapt to their environment. If there is yelling and a tense atmosphere, your dog will likely avoid spending time with you. Try to make your home a peaceful haven not just for you and your family but also for the welfare of your Maltipoo.

Shelter

Your home is the ideal habitat for your Maltipoo because it is a warm, cozy and comforting environment, but the main reason your home is ideal for your Maltipoo is because you live there.

Maltipoos don't require too much space, so they are happy living in a small apartment or having a small yard. The most important thing for them is your presence to help them feel safe and secure.

Maltipoo pups need to be with you and not locked in the laundry room or in crate. If your lifestyle means you will be leaving your Maltipoo alone for hours at a time daily, you should probably reconsider. They are prone to separation anxiety, which can cause them to create mayhem throughout your house.

Food

Maltipoos are incapable of providing for themselves. They need you to cater to their nutritional needs daily. You will need to provide a healthy, wholesome diet and fresh water.

Also, some smaller dogs have a tendency to have food allergies; you might need to adapt the diet to keep your dog healthy. You need to watch its weight, since indoor dogs sometimes eat out of boredom, and can quickly gain weight.

Love

All domesticated animals respond to love just as we humans do. Love makes us feel safe and secure. You know what makes you feel loved, but how can you show your Maltipoo that you love it?

Ear rubs make your dog go into a trance, making it look like it is high on love. Actually, that is exactly what is happening! Your dog's ears are full of nerve endings that send out endorphins when they are rubbed, and make it feel loved.

Feeding your dog by hand is an intimate way of bonding with your Maltipoo, especially when it is still a puppy. It shows that you care and says that you approve of its behavior.

Tell your dog you love it. It might not understand your words but it understands the tone of your voice.

Is a Maltipoo puppy for you?

This chapter described the ideal family for a Maltipoo puppy. If you have a warm heart with lots of love to share, then a Maltipoo could be for you. They don't need much space and are very happy living in apartment buildings if you take them for frequent short walks.

You also learned how to successfully introduce your little bundle of joy to your other dogs. Later you will learn how to take into consideration their territorial instincts and make introductions by their sense of smell.

Maltipoo pups are also a great choice for first-time dog owners. They are very easy to train and aim to please. They thrive with seniors or with families who have older children that will handle them carefully.

Maltipoo pups love to cuddle and are very sensitive to their owners' needs. Do you appreciate a good cuddle and can you give your Maltipoo the companionship it needs? If so, then a Maltipoo is the dog for you.

Maltipoos can steal your heart in a matter of seconds and you will understand why they are rapidly becoming one of the world's most popular dogs.

CHAPTER THREE
How to prepare your house for your Maltipoo puppy

Did you know that 90 percent of household pets in America live inside our houses?

Some might have free run of the house or maybe just up to a certain point. Your Maltipoo should have free run of the house once it is potty trained. But puppies love to explore and can at times get themselves into a mess.

Bringing a little puppy into your house is like bringing a toddler into a china shop. The chances of them breaking something are almost 99 percent. How can you puppy-proof your home before the puppy gets there?

Photo Courtesy of Meredith Edwards

How to puppy-proof your home

It is important to puppy-proof your house before you bring your adorable Maltipoo home and it begins to sniff out trouble. All puppies have the tendency to investigate their surroundings by touching, chewing and tasting. If you don't take precautions, some of your valuable belongings can be destroyed in a matter of minutes.

Also, as puppies continue growing, this desire to explore doesn't disappear. Some household items could cause them damage if swallowed and might even be toxic for them. Almost everything that should be kept away from a toddler should be kept away from your Maltipoo puppy.

This is a list of some of the basic steps to take; you might find you need to add some items, since every household is unique.

Trash

Keep your trash out of sight. Dogs have an excellent sense of smell, and the temptation to explore the bouquet of smells proceeding from your trash can will be too great for your little puppy to resist. If it is in plain sight, make sure it has a tight lid on it and that it is too heavy for your little Maltipoo to push over.

Electrical outlets and cords

Puppies just love to lick electrical outlets. Before you bring your puppy home, invest in some covers for your outlets. Also, be sure the electrical cords are out of sight or secured against the wall so your puppy won't be tempted to chew on them.

Furniture and other decor

Any ornaments or other items that your Maltipoo could accidently knock over or chew on should be placed on high shelves. Keep all of your shoes in the closet; they are a favorite item for Maltipoos to chew on because of all of the exotic smells and the taste of leather. Secure lamps that can easily be knocked over if your Maltipoo crashes into the table. Also any baskets, etc. that normally sit on the floor should be moved to a safer area.

Secure any dangling blind and curtain cords so they are out of reach. Your curious Maltipoo could accidently choke itself on these. In your bathroom, remember to keep your toilet lid down. A puppy could jump up there and fall in and drown.

Medications

Puppies can easily chew up anything, including childproof lids, and quickly devour anything that comes out of the containers. Before bringing your Maltipoo home, put all toiletries and medicine out of reach.

Cleaning supplies

Cleaning supplies can be toxic to humans and even more so to your tiny Maltipoo puppy. Secure all your cleaning supplies in cabinets. If you have spills, be quick to clean up so little Fido doesn't get a chance to step in it or lick it.

Backyard

If you have a backyard, make sure there are no small holes in the fence that your Maltipoo could slip through. You would be surprised how little space they need to crawl under. Secure the fence and make sure there are no sharp or dangerous items that could hurt your puppy.

Plants

Many houseplants, such as philodendrons, lilies, mistletoe, poinsettia and tomato plants, are toxic to dogs. Make sure that they are out of your Maltipoo's reach, because if it chews on their leaves, it could be serious or even fatal.

Stairs and balconies

If you have a stairwell or stairs, make sure there is a gate in place to prevent your puppy from either going up or down the stairs. It could accidently fall and fracture a bone. Also, too much stress on its developing bones could cause permanent damage that could affect its hips and knees in the future.

Close off any access to the balcony or high decks since little puppies can easily fall through openings in the railing.

Compost

If you have a compost pile in your backyard, make sure your puppy can't access it, especially if you are throwing your coffee grounds in there. Coffee grounds contain caffeine that can be toxic for dogs even in small amounts.

Prepare thoroughly

These are some simple things you can do to prepare your house or apartment for the big day when you bring your Maltipoo puppy home. These tips will help keep your four-pawed best friend safe and sound, so it can live a long and happy life by your side.

Do a walk-through of your house; or even better, get down on your knees and crawl through your house. This will bring you down to your puppy's level and you will be able to see what dangers there are down at puppy height.

A few days before you bring your new Maltipoo puppy home, give your house a thorough cleaning and check that there are no breakable items at puppy level.

House rules and routines

66 *Maltipoos are very adaptable to any home that gives them love and attention. They are very good with children that are gentle with them and also great for empty nesters."*

Renee Banovich
aTender1sPuppies.com

Rules and routines are important to maintain order and peace in the household. When you bring your new Maltipoo home, it will try to figure out where it fits in.

Consistency is the key to help your new Maltipoo to quickly settle in and begin to be part of the family.

Your rules and routine will reflect your personality and the type of relationship that you will have with your Maltipoo. The best kind of relationship to have with your dog is one that is based on mutual trust, respect and love. The key to that is to avoid, at all times, harsh verbal correction and physical punishment. As we have learned, Maltipoos are very sensitive and being treated like this will cause them to have deep emotional issues.

Before you bring your Maltipoo home, make sure you and your family discuss and agree upon the following issues:

Where will your Maltipoo sleep?

It is recommended that it sleep in a confined space close to where someone else is sleeping. Maltipoo pups are very social and get easily distressed when left alone.

Will you allow your Maltipoo on the furniture?

By cuddling with your Maltipoo on the couch, you are teaching it that it is allowed to be on the furniture. Make sure everyone is in agreement with letting your new puppy sit on the couch, etc. Some people decide that it is fine for the dog to get on the couch, but teach it to ask permission beforehand.

*Photo courtesy of
Joanna Howard*

Where will your Maltipoo be during the day?

Maltipoo owners that are retired or work from home or have the luxury of taking their dog to work with them won't have to leave their dog alone. This allows for direct supervision during the first week with regular bathroom breaks. If your pup will be left alone during the day, you might need to consider hiring a puppy sitter for the first week to take it out for potty breaks.

What games will you allow your Maltipoo to play?

Some games reinforce bad behavior such as jumping up on people, biting or barking. Be sure the whole family is in agreement about the games they can play with your Maltipoo.

Who will feed your Maltipoo, what will they feed it, and when?

Maltipoos need a regular schedule for eating. Until they are four months old, they will need to eat four times a day, then from four months to twelve months they will eat three meals a day. You will need to decide when it will be fed each of its meals. It is also important to decide who will be feeding your Maltipoo, to avoid overfeeding or forgotten meals.

Last, you will need to decide what type of dog food you will feed your Maltipoo. If it is a commercial brand, make sure it only contains whole foods and no artificial preservatives that can upset your puppy's tummy.

Who will train your Maltipoo?

Everyone in the house can take part in training your Maltipoo. It might be smart to choose a primary trainer, but everyone can participate in training your pup, since it will be part of the family. Decide beforehand tricks and behavior that you would like your pup to learn. Make a list of keywords for each one and post it on the fridge, so everyone will be using the same behavior cues, such as "go potty."

How will you correct your Maltipoo for its mistakes?

Permissiveness is every dog's worst enemy. Make sure the whole family understands how to discipline your Maltipoo. When it makes a mistake, calmly interrupt your Maltipoo's behavior with a firm but kind "no" and then redirect its attention to something else.

Puppies will develop their habits in the first few months. Don't give your Maltipoo the chance to chew on your cushions now so it will never know what it is missing when it gets older. Replace bad behavior with positive behavior.

Having a pet is a big responsibility. The way you teach your Maltipoo the house rules will allow your pet to spend the rest of its life happily sharing its loving companionship with you. Your Maltipoo deserves a loving home, so make sure your rules will provide that for your puppy.

Supplies to have on hand

Families spend months preparing for the arrival of a new baby. A new puppy doesn't need as much preparation, but it does take some organization before the big day when you bring home your baby Maltipoo puppy.

How can you make your Maltipoo comfortable as it adapts to its new environment and living with you? You need to gather some supplies for the arrival of your new puppy. What should you have before bringing home your Maltipoo?

- **Collar and leash**: Choose a collar that will be able to hold your dog's license and ID. You should be able to put two fingers under the collar. Your Maltipoo will most likely outgrow its first collar quickly. The leash should be sturdy and well made. It should be at least four feet long. As your puppy grows, you might decide to invest in a longer leash.

- **Crates and puppy den**: An expandable exercise pen, playpen or gated area that will be able to confine your puppy from roaming around the house is a good idea. If you have decided to crate train your Maltipoo, make sure the crate will be big enough for your puppy to stand up and turn around in when it is full-grown.

- **Bedding**: From day one your new Maltipoo puppy will need a soft, comfy area to lay its head. At your local pet supply store, you can find bumper beds covered with fleece and sheepskin to keep your puppy toasty warm while it is dozing away.

- **Food and water bowls**: Choose ceramic or stainless steel bowls; avoid plastic bowls that have red dye, as it can irritate your Maltipoo's eyes. Have the bowls filled up with fresh water and food so your pup can have a drink or a bite to eat when it arrives at your house.

- **Food and treats**: Your Maltipoo puppy might be very small but it has a big appetite. All growing creatures need food that will aid in their growth and development. Your puppy needs a diet that provides adequate nutrition for its rapid growth phase. Make sure to review dietary recommendations with your veterinarian to make sure the food you have chosen is right for your Maltipoo.

- **Grooming supplies**: Your Maltipoo will need to be brushed daily; the sooner you begin to brush it, the better it will behave when being groomed. In the beginning, you will need a good brush designed for the type of fur your puppy has. Brushing helps to keep your puppy's coat healthy and shiny.

- **Toys**: Puppies that are teething have sore gums, which makes them want to chew everything in sight. If you don't have enough chew toys on hand, you might as well kiss your shoes and cushions goodbye. Look for chew toys at your pet supply store that are appropriate for the type and age of dog you have. Monitor your puppy closely when it is chewing and immediately discard any toys that it has destroyed. A popular toy is a Kong chewing toy that can have treats placed inside.

- **Cleaning supplies**: Cleaning supplies are one of the main things you will need to have on hand from day one. There are plenty of cleaners on the market that are considered to be pet safe. Look for enzymatic cleaners that will break down the proteins in dog urine that send a message to your puppy to go the bathroom on the same spot. This will help prevent future accidents.
- **Litter box and doggy litter**: If you will be litter box training your Maltipoo, make sure you have plenty of newspaper on hand as you make the transition from the newspaper to the litter box. You should use doggy litter, since puppies will try to eat kitty litter, which can be toxic for them.

Photo Courtesy of
Bonnie L Braud

Service providers

It is never too soon to begin researching the different service providers that you will need to help raise your adorable Maltipoo puppy. You will need to find a veterinarian, a groomer, and if needed, a training instructor, boarding kennel, pet sitter, dog walker or doggie daycare.

How can you find information about the above?

One way is an internet search. You will be able to see all the professionals in each field in your area in a matter of seconds. Many websites offer referrals and reviews about the company.

A second option, word of mouth, is by far the best, as it is based on trustworthy opinions of those you trust. Ask your neighbors and friends whom they recommend for a certain service. Also, asking on social media can give you an endless amount of feedback to help choose the best person for the job at hand.

A third option is to scroll through the yellow pages.

The best way to decide if a service provider is for you is to pick up your phone and call them. If the provider isn't friendly on the phone, chances are they won't be pleasant in person or to your puppy. Cross them off and move on to the next name.

If they passed your telephone test, ask if you can visit to ask some questions and see them at work.

When you go visit them, observe how they treat their human and canine clients. Do they treat them with respect and care? Do the dogs look relaxed and comfortable or stressed? Are the facilities neat and tidy, with no offensive odor? Take notes and cross off the service providers that don't meet your expectations.

Once you have picked your favorite service providers, make a list of them and put it in a safe place. It would be wise to go ahead and call the veterinarian to make an appointment for your puppy's first check-up.

The journey home

The big day is here, the day to go and pick up your Maltipoo puppy and bring it home. You might be overwhelmed with joy and happiness, but how does your Maltipoo feel?

It most likely isn't excited about the big day. You are taking it away from everything it has known, its den and its family. This can be very stressful for your eight-week-old Maltipoo.

If you are well-prepared for this big day, you can make the journey to its new home a bonding experience and put its mind at ease.

Before you pick it up

Make plans to have time off from work starting the day you bring your puppy home. You will need about five to seven days to be able to properly potty train your Maltipoo and avoid bad habits taking root.

Try to bring it home during a long weekend or your vacation. This will allow for proper introductions, socialization and potty training. Avoid bringing your new puppy home during the holidays, when the festivities will interfere with giving your puppy much-needed attention.

Ask a friend or family member to come along to pick up your Maltipoo. Have your friend drive the car, while you take care of your puppy.

It is also a good idea to have a second set of ears there listening to the instructions the breeder gives you. With all the excitement, it is so easy to forget something important.

Write down beforehand any questions you might have, such as the puppy's feeding schedule and general care. Keep the list with you, so you don't forget to ask.

Ask the breeder not to feed your puppy on the day you plan to pick it up. It is common for puppies to experience carsickness and an empty stomach is the best way to prevent this.

If you plan to bring your puppy home in a crate, make sure the breeder has the crate and introduces it to your puppy a few days before your arrival. This will make the experience less traumatic.

At the breeder or shelter

Request a few days' worth of the puppy food your puppy is used to. A sudden change in diet can upset your puppy's stomach or cause it to lose its appetite. You can slowly mix the old food in with the new brand of puppy food and this will help to make an easy transition.

Collect all the necessary paperwork. Make sure you receive the adoption contract, any veterinary records and any other documentation the breeder promised.

Arrive early to your appointment. You should spend ten to fifteen minutes playing with your new puppy to introduce yourself. This will help your puppy be at ease on the drive home because at least it will know your smell.

The car ride home

This is likely your puppy's first time in a car. Let it explore the car first by smelling it. This might take a couple of minutes but you want your new puppy to trust you from day one and this is all part of the trust process.

If possible, sit in the back seat with your new puppy. Cover your lap and the upholstery with a towel or blanket, just in case your puppy gets carsick.

If your puppy begins to cry or whine, don't be overly affectionate as that will just reinforce the behavior. Just pet it softy and let it relax. If it becomes unruly and too noisy, place it on the floor between your feet. This will be like a den, helping it calm down.

If it is a long trip home, stop for bathroom breaks, being cautious not to visit bathroom spots that have been frequented by other dogs. Your little puppy hasn't been vaccinated yet, so it is susceptible to different type of diseases.

Upon arrival at your house

Once you arrive at your house, it is time to introduce your puppy to its new surroundings. First impressions last, so make sure your home is as relaxed and stress-free as possible.

The most important thing to know is that it is too soon to punish your puppy. Your puppy is overwhelmed and frightened. Punishing it will just cause confusion and stress.

First, take it to the area that you picked out for going to the bathroom. Most likely, it will need to go to the bathroom after the long car ride. If it goes on the designated spot, praise it, and voila! You have begun to potty train your Maltipoo.

When you bring your Maltipoo indoors, let it explore of its own free will. If it begins to gnaw or chew on the cushions or furniture, quickly distract it with a chew toy.

Whenever it looks at you, say its name in a cheerful manner. This teaches it its name and that you are its pack leader.

Give it something to eat and just enjoy the newest member of your family, your adorable Maltipoo puppy. It will soon become the most loyal friend of your life.

Introducing your Maltipoo to other pets

How can you introduce your new Maltipoo to your other dogs?

First, you need to know how your older dog is likely to act, so you aren't surprised by its reaction. Older dogs will not welcome the new puppy with open paws; they might growl and snub the new Maltipoo pup, but they probably will not hurt it.

Territorial instincts come into play when a new dog is introduced into the house. These territorial instincts are the main reason dogs need to meet each other on their own terms and not ours. Humans depend on sight to make judgment calls, but dogs rely heavily on their sense of smell. It is best if they can smell each other before the actual face-to-face meeting.

How can you introduce them by using their sense of smell? By following these four simple suggestions:

1. First introduction: Put each dog in a separate room, or their crates in different rooms, but put an item (such as a blanket or toy) that belongs to the other dog in the enclosed area with each one. The dogs feel very safe in their enclosed areas, and are allowed to smell the scent of the other dog without feeling intimidated. After a short time, switch the articles back to the original owner, so they can communicate by smell.

2. Second introduction: Let the new dog roam around the house. This allows it to take in its new surroundings and smell its new environment. It will be able to smell the other dog's scent around the house. While it walks around the house, it is leaving its scent around for the other dog to smell. It is very important during this step that the other dog is out of sight. After putting the new dog away, bring out the other dog, so it can smell the new scent.

3. Third introduction: Switch up the dogs. Take each one to the other dog's resting place and let them rest there, with more smells to take in and get to know. Also, when you take each dog outside to use the bathroom, let it smell the area where the other one normally goes to the bathroom. This is quality scent time.

4. Fourth meeting: Finally, the big moment comes, when they meet face-to-face. For territorial reasons, it is preferable to have the meeting on neutral ground. Perhaps you can use your neighbor's backyard or any enclosed area that is free of their scents. As they have already been formally introduced by scent, normally they will just run up to greet and smell each other, with no signs of wanting to fight.

This is a stress-free method of introducing your dogs because you are working hand in hand with the dogs' natural instincts. You could do the process in one day, but normally it works better over several days.

You need to remember that your house belonged to your older dog first, so it has some rights. How would you feel if someone you didn't know walked into your house without your permission and made themselves comfortable? You would be very disturbed and upset. Now, imagine how your older dog feels. There is a strange new dog in the house and the family is giving this new dog attention, which it never had to share before. It has the right to be upset, so be patient with your older dog and reassure it that you still love it just as much as before.

Growls are a form of communication that older dogs use but little pups haven't learned to use properly yet. New puppies might have missed some more subtle signals, such as the older dog walking away, curling in a ball, etc. The growl is the only way the puppy can learn that the older dog doesn't want to interact.

If your older dog growls at your little pup, don't be quick to punish the older dog. It is just communicating and it is a sign for you that it is time to separate the dogs for awhile, which gives them a much-needed break from each other.

It normally takes about three weeks for older dogs to accept a new dog. Just as with family, not everyone is our cup of tea; not all dogs become best friends. If this is the case with your dogs, don't be disappointed. There is enough love in the house to go around and all your dogs will feel loved and cared for.

Here are some reminders of what not to do when introducing your new Maltipoo to your older dog:

- Do not hold your new dog in your arms while making introductions. This will make the new dog feel insecure and helpless. Let the dogs meet at their own level, on the ground. You can be standing nearby, so the new dog can hide between your legs if it feels scared. But don't pick up the new dog until the introduction is completed.

- Do not let your older dog bully the new puppy. If that happens, it is time to separate the two of them for a while.

- Never lock the two dogs together in a room or crate, thinking they will work out their differences and become friends. How would you feel if you were locked in a confined space with someone you didn't know? It is a recipe for disaster.

- All dogs' instincts come into play when it is mealtime. They need to protect their food. Never put meal dishes side by side; place them on separate sides of the room. By doing this, you will be avoiding fights and they will learn to only eat from their own dishes.

- "Let them fight it out" is the worst advice in the world for humans and dogs. Ask yourself how you feel about someone you have had a verbal fight with. Do you feel like you worked out your differences, or do you feel like there is more baggage in the relationship than before? Most likely, the latter.

Dogs might have short memories but allowing them to fight teaches them that that behavior is acceptable and the new dog can begin to feel bullied and insecure, leading to anxiety. Anxiety leads to behavior problems and difficulty learning.

If you find your dogs are having difficulty accepting each other inside of your house, get outside to a neutral environment. Go for a walk around the block, with both dogs on different leashes. On the walk, both dogs will most likely go to the bathroom, allowing the other dog to smell their urine. This can be an icebreaker for most dogs.

For the first two weeks, try not to leave the dogs alone together and always be present when they are interacting. Do not leave them alone together until you are positive they have accepted each other.

It is important to continue with your older dog's normal routine, as it has established habits. Make sure you take it on its daily walks, feed it, and play with it at the same times you normally would have before the new family member arrived. This will help your older dog feel that the new dog isn't interrupting its everyday life.

CHAPTER FOUR
Potty training

Yory ou have finally found the world's most adorable Maltipoo puppy, but the day you bring it home is the beginning of a new challenge. Nobody likes waking up in the morning and seeing a mess on the
dining room carpet. Suddenly, your little Maltipoo isn't so adorable.

It normally takes less than a week to potty train your Maltipoo. It
might have an occasional accident after those seven days but it will be
a rare occurrence. Maltipoos have a very fast metabolism which means
they will need to go the bathroom more often than a larger dog.

What if you have adopted an older Maltipoo and it hasn't been correctly potty trained?

It will be more of a challenge, but the suggestions found in this chapter can also help to successfully potty train an older Maltipoo. It might
take more than seven days, plus lots of patience and love with your old-

Photo Courtesy of
Valentina Hartman

er Maltipoo as it learns new habits. You will see that you can teach an old dog new tricks, especially with potty training.

There is a famous quote that states: "My attitude is based on how you treat me."

Your Maltipoo will respond to how you treat it. If you treat it kindly, patiently and lovingly, it will respond in the same manner. But if you are nervous and visibly upset when it has its little accidents, it will become nervous and confused.

Be prepared from day one

There are entire books dedicated to how to potty train your dog, but in this chapter we focus on how to efficiently potty train your Maltipoo. You will find the suggestions in this chapter to be useful for potty training almost any dog but especially your very clever Maltipoo.

Here is a list of items that you should have on hand before you bring your Maltipoo pup home to begin potty training:
- **Treats**: It would be wise to purchase puppy biscuits or treats before you bring your Maltipoo home. Once it is there, you won't have extra time to run to the store and buy some. If you have opted to make your own homemade treats for your Maltipoo, again it is wise to make them beforehand.

  Treats can be used as rewards for when it goes to the bathroom in the designated area. This will help teach it that it is rewarded for positive behavior and it will want to repeat the process to receive a treat.
- **Squeaky toy**: This can be useful when you notice that it is about to go the bathroom, since it will distract it and stop it from going the bathroom.
- **Litter box**: If you will be potty training your Maltipoo to use a litter box, make sure you have a box which will be the correct size for your Maltipoo pup when fully grown. Have the box ready with new litter inside. It is wise to put newspaper around the box, in case it has an accident before reaching the box.

  Along with the litter box and litter, you will need a poop scooper for removing the dried poop.
- **Baby gates**: Secure baby gates will help keep your Maltipoo pup from wandering into areas of your house where you don't want it to be until potty trained.
- **Plastic bags**: Oblong bags, such as those used for newspapers or loaves of bread, are very useful for picking up your pup's poop.

- **Cleaning supplies**: Look for cleaning products that are specially designed to clean up puppy accidents in your house. They will destroy the scent that is left behind when your puppy goes to the bathroom.

- **Leash and collar**: Make sure you get a leash that is at least six feet long; it will allow your Maltipoo the space needed to find a perfect spot to eliminate while keeping it tethered so it can't run away.

- **Doggie jacket or sweater**: If you will be potty training your pup outside in the cold winter months, this will keep it warm and cozy while it takes its sweet time finding the ideal spot to go the bathroom.

  Make sure you have a warm jacket or sweater too, as Maltipoo puppies love to explore their spot thoroughly before actually going the bathroom. Also, a large umbrella is useful to keep you and your Maltipoo dry in the rain.

- **Black light**: A handy device that helps to show urine stains, which are otherwise invisible to humans. This will help you be able to efficiently clean up any messes correctly, avoiding future accidents in the same area.

- **Fencing**: If you have a backyard where you plan to let your Maltipoo roam freely, make sure the fence has no holes that your Maltipoo can crawl through and escape. Also, make sure it is high enough to keep other dogs out.

- **Crate**: If you will be crate training your Maltipoo, make sure the crate is large enough for your dog to comfortably stand up, turn around and lie down in. Take into consideration the estimated size of your Maltipoo pup when fully grown.

Also, before you begin to potty train your Maltipoo, you need to make sure you have the correct attitude from day one; otherwise, both you and your puppy will suffer. Here are some suggestions on how to get into the proper frame of mind for potty training.

Time and patience

The process of training your Maltipoo isn't going to miraculously happen overnight. The first step in preparing for bringing home your new Maltipoo pup is to prepare your attitude. You need to realize that you will need to dedicate time and energy to your little puppy. At times you will need to be extremely patient with it.

All puppies have extremely fast digestive systems; the rule of thumb is the smaller the puppy, the faster the digestive system. Maltipoos are no exception. They will need to go to the bathroom shortly after eating or drinking.

The first week will be about teaching your Maltipoo to go the bathroom in its designated spot, whether in the litter box or outside. This means you will be running your pup to the designated spot more than ten times a day. This will take time, but it will pay off in the end when your pup automatically heads to its designated spot to go to the bathroom.

Patience comes into play during the first week, when you wake up to a crying pup that wants to go the bathroom. If you are potty training outside, this might mean standing in the pouring rain at 2 a.m., while your pup tediously chooses the correct spot to go the bathroom. But remember, your puppy is learning to control its bodily functions, so this is just temporary. After a few days, it will be able to control its bladder for the whole night and there will be no more nights like this.

Positivity

" *When they have an accident, never yell, but let them know you are unhappy. They want to please you!"*

Dena Fidanza

www.denasdoggies.com

We have all experienced the following: we are trying to do something under the watchful eye of our superior. They begin to get irritated and upset with us because it is taking too long. How do we feel under that pressure? It makes us become stressed and nervous, which leads to us making a mistake.

Now how does your Maltipoo pup feel when you are watching it crossly and speaking harshly to it?

It feels the same way you would. It makes it feel nervous and stressed out, because it is still learning to control its bladder, and the stress can make it spontaneously go to the bathroom. Or worse yet, the stress causes it to forget that it needs to go to the bathroom, so it doesn't go. Then when you go back inside the house, it has an accident because it can't hold it in any longer.

Stress and negativity are contagious.

When your Maltipoo is looking for the perfect spot to do its deed, you don't want to add more pressure by telling it to hurry up or pushing it into the position. While your pup is looking for the ideal spot, be nonchalant and don't talk to it, just let it concentrate on the job at hand.

Some Maltipoo pups are shy about going to the bathroom in front of others, so you might have to look away and give it some privacy.

The key is to make it feel at ease when it is bathroom time. Some things in life just can't be rushed, so avoid rushing or stressing your puppy.

Stay calm and never, ever yell at your Maltipoo pup. If you feel like you are wasting your time for it to go to the bathroom, just remember, if you don't take the time now to properly potty train your Maltipoo pup, you will be wasting lots of time in the future cleaning up after it. So try to enjoy this bonding time with your puppy.

To correctly potty your Maltipoo you must be:
- Patient
- Calm
- Persistent and consistent
- Positive
- Respectful
- Firm

Remember, all dogs are very sensitive to our attitude; they hear it in our tone of voice and by observing our body language. If you have a bad attitude towards potty training, the puppy will pick up on it and most likely will misbehave.

Take time off from work for the first week, so you will be there to give your Maltipoo pup the much-needed time to be properly potty trained. If you are unable to take time off from work, you can hire a puppy sitter to be there when you are not there.

How to potty train your Maltipoo

Your little Maltipoo puppy has a very busy lifestyle: it eats, sleeps, plays and relieves itself. Such a hard life!

Understanding your puppy's routine and habits can aid you in successfully potty training your puppy.

Clockwork

Let's begin with understanding how the digestive system works. Normally, five to twenty minutes after your Maltipoo eats, its food is going to have to come out. That's pretty fast! By controlling eating times, you can control bathroom habits.

If it is still a puppy, it needs to eat more times during the day than a larger dog. Your Maltipoo pup's tummy is quite small and it has a faster metabolism. This is a key factor in potty training. Once you set up a regular feeding schedule, like clockwork, you can maintain regular bathroom breaks to the designated spot, soon after eating.

Maltipoo puppies need to eat about three to four times a day. Try to plan meals around the time you will be able to take it outside.

Remember that what goes in must come out. So learn to work with your puppy's digestive tract and you just might not experience any accidents in your house.

Routine

" *We begin the puppies with paper training and within 1 week, we are taking the puppies outside for regular potty breaks. It is important that the puppies always have a place to go that is away from their bedding and play areas. They want to stay clean. Puppies need a schedule for eating and potty breaks."*

Rebecca Posten

riversidepuppies.biz

Maltipoo pups love routine. They eagerly want to fit into our lifestyle and our family. The sooner they understand their schedule and where they belong, the faster they will settle into their new home, making potty training easier.

From day one, they need to know their sleeping area, water dish, food dish and the designated area to go the bathroom. Once they understand that everything has a place, potty training will not be such a big challenge.

On average, Maltipoo pups need to go to the bathroom eight to ten times per day. As soon as possible, set up a routine and begin to train your puppy that it can only go to the bathroom at certain times.

Just before you go to bed at night, take your pup to its designated spot to go to the bathroom. What if it is peacefully sleeping? Just pick it up and take it to the designated spot and wait till it does its deed. This is teaching it to adapt to your routine and helps avoid waking up in the middle of the night to a crying puppy that needs to go the bathroom.

Likewise, when you wake up in the morning, before making your cup of coffee, go wake your puppy up and take it to its designated spot to go to the bathroom. It most likely will want to play with you, but be patient, it is learning your schedule.

The first few days, you will most likely have to be running it to its designated spot every two hours, but little by little, those intervals will get longer and longer, as its bladder gets stronger. Before you know it, your puppy will be able to make it through the night without needing a bathroom break.

Potty training teaches your puppy that there is a set time and place for going to the bathroom, that it cannot just go wherever and whenever it wants to.

Pick the spot

You want your Maltipoo to feel safe and secure in the designated spot that you have chosen for its bathroom. Make sure it isn't too noisy and there aren't big vehicles passing by. This will just frighten your little puppy and it may not go to the bathroom.

A word of caution: Pick a spot that hasn't been used by another dog. All the smells will be overwhelming for it. Choose an area that is only for your puppy to use and it will only have its own scent left there.

When choosing the designated spot, it is important to be able to get there quickly, but avoid it being right out your front door or porch. It will most likely continue to use this spot even after it is potty trained, as the scent is telling it to return to that spot. As it continues to grow, so will the size of poop and it isn't the most pleasant thing to see as you walk up to your house. Choose a spot that is isolated but close.

If you are living in an apartment building, getting outside quickly can be quite the challenge. But as mentioned before, Maltipoo pups respond well to being litter box trained. You will need to follow the same suggestions found in this chapter, but the designated spot will be the litter box.

Introducing your puppy to the designated spot

The first thing you need to do when you bring your Maltipoo pup home is introduce it to its designated spot. It is probably tired, excited and a little stressed out. Plus, it just had a scary car ride to your house. Most likely, your new Maltipoo needs to relieve itself.

Put it down close to the designated spot. Try to allow it to walk up to the area alone, as it will feel safer. Let it check out the area. If it is outside it will smell the grass and maybe even play a little. If it doesn't go in the first five minutes, take it inside and show it the bed, water and food dish. Once it has checked out this area, take it back to its designated area again, and this time, wait till it goes to the bathroom, leaving behind its scent there. This makes it easier for it to go to the bathroom there in the future.

When should you take your Maltipoo to its spot?
- Whenever your puppy wakes up. (morning, afternoon or evenings)
- Whenever it finishes eating or having a big drink of water.
- After playing or being excited.
- If you hear it whining at night or anytime of the day.
- If it is standing at the door looking to go outside.

Helpful hints

- Puppies need to eat at least three times a day: breakfast, lunch and dinner. Try to feed your puppy at the same time every day.
- Maltipoo puppies will need to go the bathroom about ten times a day, normally when you get up and before going to bed, after meals, after playing and after a drink.
- Take your puppy to its designated spot as much as possible. After it has gone to the bathroom, reward it with some special playtime.

General potty training schedule

Have your shoes and clothes near your bed, so you will be ready to go in the morning.

MORNING	
6:00 - 6:30	Take your Maltipoo puppy outside IMMEDIATELY
7:15 - 7:30	Indoor playtime
7:30 - 8:00	Feed your puppy in its confined space (Allow 15 to 20 minutes for digestion)
8:00	Take your puppy to its designated bathroom spot
8:15	Place puppy in its confined area

AFTERNOON	
12:00	Take your puppy outside
12:15 - 12:00	Indoor playtime
12:30 - 1:00	Feed your puppy in its confined space (Allow 15 to 20 minutes for digestion)
1:00	Take your puppy to its designated bathroom spot
1:15	Place your puppy in its confined area.

EVENING	
5:00 - 5:30	Take your puppy outside
6:15 - 6:30	Indoor playtime
6:30 - 7:00	Feed your puppy in its confined space (Allow 15 to 20 minutes for digestion)
7:00 - 8:00	Take puppy outside
8:00 - 9:00	Indoor playtime
9:00	Place your puppy in its confined area
10:30 - 11:00	Take your puppy outside
11:15	Return puppy to confined area for bed time

This is just a basic guideline for potty training your Maltipoo. You can adapt it to your own schedule. Maltipoo puppies younger than four months old will need to eat four times a day, so take that into consideration when making a schedule.

Rewards and potty training

Puppies love to be rewarded for their good behavior.

Studies have shown that when animals are rewarded for good behavior, it sends a message to their brain telling them that it is beneficial to repeat this behavior. When they repeat the behavior and they are rewarded, the desire to repeat the behavior becomes stronger. After a while, it just becomes part of their normal routine and there will be no reason to reward them for the good behavior anymore.

This is exactly the aim of potty training; you want to teach your Maltipoo that going to the bathroom at its designated spot is good behavior.

When and how should you reward your Maltipoo?

The reward should be given IMMEDIATELY after it relieves itself in its designated spot. Make sure you always have some treats in your pocket to give it right away, so it will associate going to the bathroom at that spot with being rewarded and will want to repeat it.

Verbal rewards: Once it has finished going to the bathroom, get down to its level, if possible, and pat it generously, telling it that it is a good dog and it did a good job. Be very enthusiastic and positive, as you are teaching with your tone of voice that you are very pleased.

It might be difficult to show enthusiasm at 2 a.m. in the pouring rain, but it is only temporary and most likely you will only have get up that early two or three times to take your Maltipoo out to the bathroom.

Edible rewards: These will be your puppy's favorite type of reward. Give a treat while you are giving the verbal reward or encouragement.

Physical rewards: If you can, this is a wonderful time to begin to bond with your Maltipoo by playing with it outside. It will consider this to be part of the reward for relieving itself on its designated spot.

Going outside or to the litter box will be one of the highlights of your puppy's day, with all of the rewards it will be receiving. It will want to go the designated spot.

When should you not reward your Maltipoo?
- It was left home alone and had an accident in its confined space.
- It went to the bathroom while you were playing with it in the house.
- It escaped from its confined space and went to the bathroom inside of your house.

Of course, these occasions do not merit being punished, as your puppy will not understand why you are upset. But it will begin to see that bathroom time only brings rewards when it is at the designated spot. Never give your puppy a treat for bad behavior, as this will just confuse it and make potty training a hardship for both of you.

The more times your Maltipoo is rewarded for this good behavior, the faster it will be trained. This is why it is considered to be an important part of the first week of potty training. It is teaching good habits that will stick with it for life.

To crate train or to den-train

Both crate training and den training will require confining your puppy from the rest of your house, by using the door to the crate (or a baby gate for den training). When den training, the confinement area should be free of furniture and other non-dog-related items.

You can purchase an exercise pen or a playpen at most pet stores, which can be set up in any room of your house.

Place in the puppy den or the crate something soft and cuddly for it to sleep on. Also put in a water bowl and several of your puppy's favorite toys, such as a Kong stuffed with treats for your puppy.

How to get your Maltipoo used to its new confinement area:

Step 1: Take your Maltipoo outside for a walk or some serious playtime. This will get your little pup tired out, so it will eagerly go into the confinement area.

Step 2: Once you place it in its confinement area, give it a stuffed Kong or some treats. This will keep it distracted as you go about your business in your house.

Step 3: It will finish the treats in about five minutes; this is when it will realize that you have abandoned it in this confined area. It might begin to whine or cry, but just ignore it until it stops. Once it stops, you can go make a fuss over it.

Step 4: The next day, try to leave the house for a short period, such as going outside to water the plants or check the mail. As the days pass, leave the house for longer periods, normally after you have already given your puppy a bathroom break.

Repeat steps 1-3 throughout the day, gradually increasing the amount of time you leave your puppy there alone. You can start off with one minute and gradually work up to twenty minutes.

Leave your puppy in its confinement area for the night; when you hear it barking during the night, get up and take it to the bathroom.

Clean the area immediately after any accident, to avoid more accidents.

Crate training

Crate training teaches your puppy that the crate is its safe den, which should not be used for going the bathroom.

Crate training basically involves confining your puppy to the crate when it isn't playing, eating or drinking. As it is a very confined area, your Maltipoo will quickly understand that it will not be able to go the bathroom in there and it is only for sleeping.

Once you have picked out the ideal crate for your Maltipoo, you need to find the ideal location for the crate. You can have more than one location; for instance, placing the crate in your bedroom at night and during the day having the crate near where people will be.

A word of caution: Don't place the crate in direct sunlight, as this can cause your Maltipoo to become overheated, leading to heatstroke and other complications.

When introducing your Maltipoo to the crate, let it walk in alone and explore it alone. Do not force your puppy to go into the crate, as that will just frighten it.

You might need to bribe your puppy to go into the crate at first by giving it treats and toys. Pet it while it is in the crate and tell it what a good dog it is.

Try feeding your puppy while it is inside of the crate; once it seems comfortable in there, begin to close the door for short periods, while you are present.

If it begins to whine or bark to be let out, don't let it out or sweet-talk it. This is the moment that tough love comes into play. If you let your puppy out while it is crying, you are teaching it that whining is the code to be released from the crate.

Den training

Den training teaches your puppy that your whole house is its den or sleeping area.

Puppies learn from birth that they need to keep their eating and sleeping area clean, because their mother constantly cleans up after them. Dogs, like most animals, are quite smart. They know if they start pooping and peeing in their sleeping area, life is going to go downhill pretty fast. Dogs, by basic instinct, are naturally clean animals.

What is a puppy den?

A puppy den is normally a small, closed-in area that will limit the amount of accidents that your puppy has, preventing the spread of enzymes that direct your puppy to go to the bathroom repeatedly in the same spot.

A typical puppy den in your house will be a small puppy pen with an enclosed area that can expand little by little. It is preferable to place it on hard flooring instead of carpeting, for easier cleanup. It might be in your bathroom or kitchen (which has been temporarily enclosed to prevent puppy from escaping and finding new potty spots in your house).

The puppy den is just a temporary confinement space, which gradually expands, teaching your puppy that the new space is part of its sleeping quarters, so it must be kept clean. It will eventually expand to your entire house, when it understands that your house is the den and it is unacceptable to go to the bathroom there.

The puppy den should always have a dish of fresh water for your Maltipoo puppy, a sleeping area, and a food dish that it will use three to four times a day, until it is about one year old. Also, it should have some toys inside of the den to play with to avoid becoming bored.

When you put your puppy in the puppy pen, start by leaving it there for a short period. If it begins to cry or whine when you leave, don't quickly rush back to reassure it that everything is okay. This will just teach it that whining and crying is acceptable and you will come running.

Many people combine a puppy den with crate training, by using the crate as the sleeping area for their puppy. The door should be tied open, so that it can't close and lock your pup inside. Placing it in the corner of the den teaches the puppy that the crate is its friend so it can be used in the future for travelling, etc., without causing your Maltipoo added stress.

Your puppy will understand from day one that this is its safe spot. It will not want to stink up its special area by eliminating there.

Is it cruel to confine your puppy to a small area?

Some might reason that it is cruel to confine your puppy to a small area like a crate or a puppy den, but consider the whole picture. Would you let your toddler roam freely about your house unsupervised? Of course not; there are too many chances for them to get hurt or get into trouble.

The same goes for your little Maltipoo puppy. Your house, even though it has been puppy-proofed, still has an endless supply of potty spots for your puppy to make its own and it could still get hurt.

The first seven days of confining your puppy to the puppy den are essential to successfully potty training your Maltipoo pup and establishing good habits. Why is it beneficial to use a puppy den?

- This confinement is temporary and serves the purpose of teaching your puppy not to go to the bathroom inside the house. The confinement will expand a little each day, until you can trust it with the whole house.

- If allowed to roam freely about your house from day one, it would pee wherever, leaving its scent all over your house. It might seem innocent at first, but as your puppy grows, its urine gets stinky and its poop gets bigger. Also, it will learn bad habits that will be extremely hard to break later on.

- If you plan on leaving your puppy alone when it is bigger but don't take the time to properly potty train it as a puppy, you will most likely end up locking it into a smaller confined space, such as the bathroom, for hours, since you will not be able to trust it to roam around the house when left alone. Not confining your Maltipoo when it is little leads to confinement when it is bigger.

- Sadly, each year many cute puppies and dogs are euthanized because they were not properly potty trained during the first couple of weeks in their new house.

It isn't cruel to use a puppy den or a crate to potty train your Maltipoo pup, because it is temporary and because of the long-term benefits to your Maltipoo and you.

It is highly recommended to set up the crate or puppy den before you bring your new Maltipoo pup home. This will instantly teach your puppy that this is its special sleeping area, and its basic instinct is to keep that area clean.

Remember little accidents lead to bigger accidents. The key to potty training is preventing the little accidents from day one.

Pros and cons of crate and den training

Pros of crate training

1. It will give you peace of mind when you have to leave your Maltipoo pup alone for longer periods, since you know your puppy will not be using your oriental rug as its bathroom.

2. Crate training is considered to be one of the most effective methods of potty training, because the puppy is forced to learn to control its bodily functions fast, since as a basic instinct it will not want to dirty its sleeping area.

3. Crate training can help tremendously when potty training an older dog, as will be explained at the end of this chapter.

4. If you will be travelling frequently by plane or car and your puppy will need to be transported by crate, it will be less stressful as it is already accustomed to its crate.

Cons of crate training

1. Your Maltipoo pup learns that the crate is its sleeping area, so it will not pee in there, but when it is let loose in your house unsupervised it may not understand its boundaries and is likely to have an accident in your house.

2. Small dogs such as Maltipoos, when crate trained, often are more aggressive with children and unknown guests.

3. Some people consider crate training to be a form of cruelty, as the animal is locked into a small space that it cannot escape from. They reason that since you would not lock a small child in a cage and leave it alone for a couple of hours, you shouldn't do it to a dog either.

4. Crate training is not suitable for all dogs, especially dogs that have spent a lot of time in a crate or cage (such as in a shelter or with previous owners), as it may make them very agitated and upset.

5. Some Maltipoos suffer from separation anxiety and can become more upset in a crate than they would in a larger space.

6. Crate training is not natural; some reason that because dogs descended from wolves and they lived in dens it is natural. But the wolves were able to leave the den of their own free will. A crate is an artificial confinement which many people use for their own convenience. If you decide to use a crate, limit the amount of time your Maltipoo spends in the crate with the door closed.

Pros of den training

1. Small dogs that are den trained are friendlier to children and strangers than puppies that were crate trained.

2. Maltipoos that are den trained are less likely to suffer from separation anxiety, since they don't feel claustrophobic in a tight confined space.

3. Den training teaches your Maltipoo little by little that your whole house is its den, so it will not relieve itself in your house when left alone or unsupervised, once it is potty trained. By basic instinct, it will keep the den free of bathroom smells.

4. Den training is a very humane way of potty training your puppy, as it has freedom to move about and is not locked in a small cage.

5. Den training is considered to be one of the most effective ways to potty train smaller dogs which will be living inside with their owners.

It teaches the pup from day one that it is not allowed to go potty inside the house.

Cons of den training

1. When left unsupervised, your Maltipoo could push over the barrier and escape.
2. Since the confinement area is larger than a crate, there might be one or two accidents within the area. This can be quickly cleaned up to avoid future accidents.

Clean-up advice

Accidents are bound to happen. It's not the end of the world when they happen, so don't fret about it. The key to preventing future accidents is to understand the importance of properly cleaning up after your puppy makes a mess.

Basic instinct

Since the day your Maltipoo was born, it has been trained to keep itself and its area clean. Newborn Maltipoo pups do three basic things in their little den or space: eat, sleep and relieve themselves. Their mother's instincts kick in, and she is constantly tidying up their little den and her baby pups, so their little space doesn't smell like urine or feces. The pups are brought up knowing that their living quarters need to be free of bodily waste. As the pups grow, they begin to move away from their sleeping area to go the bathroom. You want them to see your whole house as part of their den or living area.

When you bring your little Maltipoo home for the first time, it doesn't understand where its bedroom ends and the bathroom area begins. Basic instincts tell it that it shouldn't make a mess where it sleeps. But how can cleaning up contribute to potty training?

Enzymes

Have you noticed how dogs are attracted to a spot where another dog went to the bathroom and then proceed to go the bathroom in that same spot?

All dogs have enzymes in the urine and feces and these enzymes are left behind even after wiping up the mess. If it hasn't been correctly cleaned up, the puppy can still smell its enzymes. These enzymes are telling it that it is fine to go the bathroom on that spot. This is why so many

Photo Courtesy of
Mary Papadopoulos

new puppy owners keep having repeat accidents in the same spot: the mess is gone but the enzymes are still there.

How can we eliminate these enzymes?

The only way is to use the right cleaning products. At your local supermarket, you can find special products that have been designed for cleaning up after your puppy. These products will rid your house of these enzymes that are inviting your puppy to go to the bathroom.

You should avoid using cleaning products that contain ammonia. Ammonia makes the enzymes smell stronger, telling your puppy to go to the bathroom there again. This is one cause of puppies always having accidents in the same area of the house.

The key to stopping your puppy from having accidents inside of your house is to take the time to clean up any messes it has made.

If you are using a litter box for potty training your Maltipoo, don't be too quick to change the litter in the beginning. We want the pup to recognize by the scent of its enzymes that it needs to do its deeds in there.

If you are teaching it to go to the bathroom outside, always take it to the same spot so it can smell the enzymes that were left behind from last time. After a week or so, it will begin to automatically go there alone.

If you have another dog, make sure that they each have their own litter box or outside spot to go the bathroom. Otherwise, instead of going to bathroom when it is time, they will become fascinated with the scent left behind by the other dog and quickly forget that they had to go to the bathroom.

How to correctly clean up after your puppy

1. Pick up the fecal matter or wipe up the urine with a paper towel. Place the paper towel into a garbage bag.

2. Spray a cleaning product designed for cleaning up after your puppy all around the area. The enzymes can be spread up to a foot around the mess, so be generous in cleaning up.

3. If your puppy accidently stepped in it, wipe off its paws with water. Do not use chemicals on its paws, as they could make it sick. Use a clean rag and the cleaning product for wherever it might have wandered.

4. If possible, use paper towels for cleanup or a new rag for each spot, as that will avoid spreading enzymes around the house.

5. Be quick when cleaning up messes, especially if the mess was made on the carpet, as the underlayment could quickly absorb it.

Dos and don'ts in potty training

When you tell your friends and family that you will be bringing home a new puppy, don't be surprised when everyone suddenly turns into an expert on potty training. But not all the advice you receive is wise to apply when potty training your Maltipoo.

Your Maltipoo is just a little baby and it is just learning how to control its bowels. Would you treat a little child badly because he or she pooped or peed their pants or bed? No, you understand it wasn't their fault and they just couldn't control themselves. The same is true for your little Maltipoo: it isn't their fault.

The worst advice that many people give is rub your dog's nose in its mess. Rubbing your dog's nose in its mess will not teach it anything, except to be afraid of you and think you are crazy. All dogs have short memories; your puppy has likely forgotten all about it.

Maltipoo dogs are very sensitive and do not respond well to yelling or things being thrown at them. It will cause anxiety and stress which will very likely lead to another accident right there, but out of fear and not necessity.

If your Maltipoo is taking a long time outside to find a perfect spot to do its deed, do not become agitated and upset with your pup. The puppy will not understand why you are upset which may cause it not to go to the bathroom, even though it has to go. Then when you go into the house, since it didn't go outside, it will go inside.

Caught in the act

What if your puppy is in the act of going to the bathroom inside the house?

Most accidents that happen inside the house are the owner's fault because they didn't get the puppy outside or to the litter box in time to go to the bathroom and its little bladder just couldn't hold it in any more.

There are some warning signs that can alert you to take your Maltipoo pup to its designated spot. If you are able to identify these warning signs you will be able to prevent accidents from happening. Here is a list of warning signs:
1. All dogs and puppies love to smell and circle around the area before they go to the bathroom there. So, if you see your Maltipoo pup intently smell a certain area and begin going around in circles, it is time to pick up your puppy and take it to its designated spot.
2. If it begins to squat, that is a sure sign that it is about to go to the bathroom. Quickly but gently pick your puppy up and hold it so its belly is against yours. That should stop it from peeing and you can

take it to its designated spot. If it already peed inside the house, it was your fault for not paying attention.

3. If your puppy begins to bark or whine while looking in the direction of its designated spot, it is probably trying to communicate with you and tell you that it needs to go to the bathroom now. Pay attention to your Maltipoo's verbal communication.

Don't get mad or yell; Maltipoos are extremely sensitive and this will cause them to get physically stressed. Most of all, remember that if your Maltipoo had an accident inside the house, it is your fault, not your puppy's. So do not get mad at your Maltipoo about the accident.

If your Maltipoo is peeing, quickly but calmly pick it up and say a firm "no." Carry it outside to its spot or to its litter box, holding its tail down between its legs to stop it from urinating. Let it finish the deed outside or in the litter box, and then praise it for being a good dog. Quickly clean up any mess that was made inside.

It is easier to stop your Maltipoo from peeing than pooping. If you notice that it is about to pee inside the house, try to distract it so it will stop peeing. The goal is to startle your puppy without scaring it. One way is to have on hand a squeaky toy that you can squeeze just as it begins to pee. This will startle it, and its natural canine curiosity is likely to cause it to stop peeing and check out the noise. This will give you time to pick up your Maltipoo pup and take it to its designated spot.

If it is caught in the act of pooping, the best thing to do is to let it finish its business. If you try to pick it up in middle of the act, all you will accomplish is making a big mess everywhere. So just let it finish, then take it outside after and clean up the mess. When cleaning up the mess, don't make a big show out of it. Your Maltipoo probably already feels bad for what it did; remember, it is just a baby.

Accidents happen

The *number one rule* with potty training your Maltipoo is: if you didn't catch your puppy in the act, don't punish your puppy. Don't even talk to your puppy about it. Just clean it up.

When your puppy successfully does its deed in the designated spot, take the time to reward it. It is not necessary to reward with a biscuit or a snack; the best reward is your time and praise. Take the time to play with your puppy and tell it how proud you are of it for being such a good dog.

You want your puppy to associate being rewarded with good behavior such as going to the bathroom in its designated spot. Here is a list of instances when you shouldn't reward your Maltipoo pup with treats or verbal praise.

- It was home alone and had an accident in its puppy den or crate.
- It was caught in the act but you caught it in time and took it to its designated area.
- It escaped from its crate or puppy den and did its dirty deed in your house.

Your Maltipoo is very intelligent and will begin to understand that rewards only come when it goes to the bathroom on a certain spot. Slowly but surely, it will begin to connect the dots and it will understand that it is beneficial to go to the bathroom at its designated spot and not on your carpet.

Never let your puppy roam about the house unsupervised or without you being home until it is fully potty trained. There are just too many temptations to find the perfect bathroom spot: behind the couch, under your bed, etc. Only let your Maltipoo roam around your house under your watchful eye.

Plan to be at home as much as possible during the first week of potty training. The more time your Maltipoo pup is alone, the greater the chance of it having an accident and spreading its enzymes around the house. This will make potty training even more difficult, as the enzyme smell basically sends a message to its brain saying, "Pee here."

Never give rewards for bad behavior; that will just confuse your Maltipoo pup and encourage bad behavior.

Spontaneous peeing

Maltipoo puppies and dogs have a tendency to lose control of their bladders when they get overly excited. It might happen while they are playing or greeting you or meeting somebody new. Don't punish them for spontaneously peeing. They can't control themselves and most likely don't even realize that they peed. As they get older, spontaneous peeing will cease.

Training your Maltipoo to use a litter box

Litter boxes seem to go hand in hand with cats; even the litter for the litter box is commonly called "kitty litter." But it is possible to buy dog litter that has been designed for dogs.

Why should you consider training your Maltipoo to use a litter box?

1. Many Maltipoo owners live in apartment buildings or condos that have little or no access to a green area for their Maltipoo to relieve itself. It is more practical to have a litter box in the house for quick and easy access which makes potty training a breeze.

2. Maltipoo pups have small bladders. Having a litter box in the house gives them the freedom to go whenever they want to. Most Maltipoo owners that have litter boxed trained their puppy have expressed that their puppy never had an accident in the house.

3. With a Maltipoo that is litter box trained, your Maltipoo will be fine wherever you travel, as long as there is a litter box. You won't be waking up to an unwanted surprise on your host's rug.

4. Your Maltipoo can use the litter box when it is alone in the house. It will still go to the bathroom when you take it on walks outside, so be sure to bring your pooper-scooper with you.

How can you train your puppy to use the litter box?

1. In the confinement area, place newspaper on the floor, if possible with a small plastic tray under it to prevent leakage.

2. Place your puppy on the spot and say "Go potty." It most likely will not go, but repeat the process of saying "Go potty" to teach it that this spot is something positive.

3. You might need to soak the newspaper in its urine from when it went outside, as the smell will attract it, sending a message to its brain that it needs to relieve itself there.

4. Watch your puppy like a hawk and when you see it about to go the bathroom, quickly pick it up and place it on the newspaper. Again tell it to "Go potty." Once it has gone on the newspaper, it will most likely go there again. Liberally praise it each time it goes potty on the newspaper.

5. Once it has gone three or four times on the newspaper, put some doggy litter on top of the newspaper. It will continue using this area for its bathroom, as its enzymes or scent are telling it to return to this designated spot. It will most likely be wary of litter in the beginning. *Repeat step 2.*

6. Once it is used to the litter and going to the bathroom on the newspaper with the litter, you can bring out the litter box that you are planning on using. Place the dirty newspaper on the bottom of the box and the litter on top. The scent and material will let your Maltipoo know that it is acceptable to go the bathroom here. *Repeat step 2.*

7. Once it is used to the new box, you can move the box about a foot each day, towards the area where the box will permanently stay in the future. Make sure the box has newspapers around it, as acci-

dents might happen en route to the box. Be quick in cleaning up after them. Every time you move the box closer to the designated spot, *repeat step 2.*

8. Once you have reached the permanent area for the box, your Maltipoo will be potty trained and will understand that the only designated area for going to the bathroom in the house is in its litter box.

Suggestions:

- Doggy litter is preferable to kitty litter, as puppies will try to eat the kitty litter. Doggy litter looks more like rabbit filler or pellets, which will turn to sawdust when wet. Doggy litter is biodegradable.

- Once you decide on a certain brand of litter, continue using that brand to avoid confusing your puppy. If you do decide to switch to kitty litter when your Maltipoo is older, begin by mixing the new kitty litter into the doggy litter.

- The litter box is not meant to replace going to the bathroom outside; it is to be used as a backup for when you can't take your Maltipoo outside. You should still set aside time to take your Maltipoo outside to play and walk every day.

- It is easier to litter box train your Maltipoo when it is still very young. It is possible with older dogs, but it will be more of a challenge.

- Try placing the litter box close to the outside door, so your Maltipoo will associate that area with going to the bathroom.

- Tiled areas are easiest to clean up, but if only carpeted areas are available, put plastic or newspaper underneath the litter box.

Before you bring home your Maltipoo puppy, purchase a litter box designed for small dogs at your local pet retailer. Depending on the size of your Maltipoo when it is full-grown, a cat box might be sufficient. If you have a male Maltipoo, it might wise to look for a litter box that has a higher side, in case of leg lifting when peeing. Make sure the entrance to the litter box is lower to the ground allowing easy access for your tiny Maltipoo pup.

Just as when outdoor potty training your Maltipoo, you should take your pup to the litter box as soon as it wakes up and before going to bed, after eating or having a big drink of water, and periodically throughout the day.

Watch carefully for any signs that it needs to go to the bathroom, such as circling, squatting or intensely smelling a certain area. When you see this type of activity, quickly but carefully pick up your Maltipoo, take it to its box, and say your command to go to the bathroom.

Whenever it goes to the bathroom in the box, enthusiastically praise it for going in the right spot. Your Maltipoo will be very eager to please you.

Dogs do not have the behavioral instincts of cats to use a litter box. It comes naturally to cats to use a litter box and bury their waste. Litter box training your puppy will take a lot of patience and energy, but it is possible. As with everything in life, we only get out of it what we put into it; the effort you put into litter box training your Maltipoo will give you peace of mind in the future.

As with all types of potty training, accidents will happen, so be prepared to clean up and have lots of patience with your baby Maltipoo.

Potty training an older dog

Many rescue dogs haven't been properly potty trained, some not at all. Other Maltipoo dogs that were at the shelter for a long time might have been potty-trained previously but will need a refresher course as they didn't get regular walks at the shelter.

The good news is that you can teach an old dog new tricks. They can be potty trained.

The key to successfully potty training an older Maltipoo is to start from the minute you bring your dog home. It is recommended to crate train an older dog for the first week, then gradually switch to den training, using the crate in the den but not closing the door.

Step one:
Take the first week off work to properly train your adult Maltipoo. Someone will need to take your adult dog out for walks or to the designated spot. The best person to do this is you, so your dog will begin to bond with you.

Step two:
Begin using the crate from day one. Crate training is a good solution for potty training your adult dog, because it won't like to soil its sleeping and eating areas.

Make sure the crate is big enough for your Maltipoo to stand up and turn around in. If it is too big, your dog might decide that there is room to go the bathroom in the corner.

Keep the crate in a high-traffic part of the house, so it doesn't feel isolated and alone.

Make sure the crate is only used when necessary; give your new dog lots of playtime, exercise and obedience training outside of the crate.

If you don't think using a crate is humane, please understand you won't have to use it for very long. Three or four days is likely all it will take before your adult dog is potty trained.

Step three:
Give your adult Maltipoo at least six to eight bathroom breaks a day.

How many times do you go the bathroom a day? Quite a few, since you know that holding it for long periods can cause bladder infections or other complications. The same goes for your Maltipoo. It needs to relieve itself at least six times a day.

It will need to go to the bathroom when you wake up and before you go to bed, and also after meals, drinking water, or playing. Once it is potty trained it may only need to relieve itself four to five times a day.

Step four.
Generously praise and reward your dog when it relieves itself in the designated area.

Praise and rewards send a message to your dog's brain, telling it that this behavior is beneficial. It will repeat the behavior in order to be rewarded again, and after time it will become a routine.

Make sure the praise and rewards come right after eliminating. You want your dog to clearly understand that eliminating in the designated spot is the best thing in the world for you. Don't wait to give the treat later, as it will not be able to associate the treat with relieving itself.

After your dog goes to the bathroom, give it some playtime as a reward. If you only take it outside for the bathroom, it will quickly learn to linger when outside before going to the bathroom, just to prolong the time outside with you.

Step five:
Never punish your dog for an accident that you did not actually see it do. If you catch your dog in the act, startle it midstream with a clap, then quickly take it to its designated spot so it can finish the job.

Clean up thoroughly so it isn't enticed to return to the same spot by the enzymes in the urine or poop.

Leave the soiled towels near its designated spot; the scent will encourage your dog to relieve itself at that spot.

When cleaning up, stay away from ammonia-based cleaners, as they smell like urine to your dog and it will want to go pee again on the same spot.

Bottom line: Crate training is a very effective way to potty train an older dog and it can be temporary. Remember to generously reward your dog whenever it goes to the bathroom on its designated spot. Punishing your dog for accidents can make potty training more tedious and longer.

Summary

Potty training your Maltipoo will take patience and lots of love, but is very easy to do if you follow the suggestions in this chapter. Normally, potty training will take less than a week to do, but there will still be an occasional accident as your pup learns to control its bodily functions.

As the old saying goes, "don't cry over spilled milk." Don't make a big deal about something that has already happened. What's done is done.

The same goes for your Maltipoo's accidents. It happened, so deal with it. Most likely, it was your fault that it happened because you weren't alert to your dog's signals. The only thing you can do is thoroughly clean up the mess and get on with your life.

Potty training is a small ordeal that will take about a week of your time. You need to have the right attitude, being patient, calm and persistent while potty training your Maltipoo puppy.

Potty training means learning to get your puppy's schedule to work around your schedule. It is very easy to do as puppies go to the bathroom like clockwork, when they wake up and before bed and after eating.

You need to pick a designated spot where you want it to relieve itself. You should choose a spot that you can reach quickly, that hasn't been used by another dog.

Potty training will only take a few days out of your busy lifestyle, but the result will be that you have a well-behaved dog that you can let roam around your house worry-free. Take the time to apply the suggestions found in this chapter when potty training and you will have the best-behaved dog on the block.

CHAPTER FIVE
Obedience training

Maltipoo dogs are one of the easiest dogs to train because of their intelligence, good temperament and eagerness to please their owners. But sadly, most Maltipoo pups are spoiled rotten little brats. Why is that?

How to train your Maltipoo

The problem lies not with the good-tempered Maltipoo but with its owners. They did not take the time to properly train it. As with children, if parents don't take the time to correct bad behavior, it will soon turn into habits and finally become part of their personality. These personality traits become deep-rooted and almost impossible to correct later on in life. The same occurs with your moldable Maltipoo puppy. You can mold it by obedience training positively or negatively; it all depends on how much effort you are willing to invest into training.

Spoiled rotten brats are a reflection of their parents. Normally when we see a disobedient child throwing a tantrum, we instantly think the mother is to blame and we might ask ourselves: *"Why doesn't she teach her child how to behave better?"*. The same rule of thumb applies to your Maltipoo dog, how it behaves depends upon one factor: YOU!

One of the reasons that Maltipoo owners don't properly train their puppies is due to their size. They look so innocent and cute that it breaks their owners' hearts to discipline them. But that adorable little puppy can turn into an irritating spoiled rotten brat in no time.

Also, because of their size, their owners often do not feel the need to train them, as they pose no threat when compared to a larger dog. But remember, no matter what size dog you have--tiny, small or large--all dogs can deliver a bite that is dangerous to humans and might require stitches. Any dog, no matter its size, can run away from you right into traffic or into a crowd.

As with most things in life, the results will reflect how much time you were willing to invest. This is especially true for training your dog. You need to realize that from the very first day that you bring your Maltipoo home, you will be spending the next few months training your dog.

*Photo Courtesy of
Karin Dixon*

Training your dog will include potty training, obedience training, leash training, how to interact with other people and dogs, and so much more. Training your dog allows you to bond with your Maltipoo and develop a loving relationship with it.

By taking the time to properly train your Maltipoo dog, you are ensuring its safety and the safety of those around it.

Four basic commands to teach your Maltipoo

These are some basic commands that you will need to teach your Maltipoo. Teaching your puppy these commands will help prevent behavioral issues later on. All of these commands can be taught by you. The key is having the right attitude, making it a fun, bonding time for the both of you.

Sit

This is one of the easiest and most important commands to teach your Maltipoo.

1. Show your Maltipoo a treat and hold it up to its nose.
2. Slowly, move your hand up above its head. It will follow the treat with its head and sit down.
3. Once it is sitting, say the key word "sit," then give the treat and generously praise it.
4. Repeat steps 1 through 3 a few times during the day, until your Maltipoo has mastered it. Then begin to ask your dog to sit before going for walks, mealtime and any other situation. Make sure you always praise it for sitting when asked.

Come

This is another common command that you will frequently use to call your Maltipoo, to keep it from going too far or to avoid unfortunate accidents.

1. Put your dog's leash and collar on.
2. Get down to its level and say, "come." At the same time, gently pull on the leash to bring it towards you.
3. When it comes to you, give it a treat and generously praise it.
4. Repeat steps 1 through 3 until it has mastered the command. Then begin to practice without the leash; of course, always practice in a safe, enclosed area where your Maltipoo can't run away.

Down

This is one of the trickiest commands to teach your Maltipoo, but you will be so grateful if both of you master it, as it will save you much heartache later on. It is considered to be difficult because the dog by natural instinct considers it to be an act of submissiveness. Try to keep a relaxed attitude with your Maltipoo while teaching this command.

1. Choose your pup's favorite treat and hold it inside of your closed fist. Make sure it has a strong smell.

2. Hold your fist up to your Maltipoo's nose so it can smell the treat. Then move your hand to the floor. Its head will follow your hand to the floor.

3. Once its head is close to the floor, slide your hand along the ground in front of it. This will encourage it to be in a semi-sitting laying position, with all four legs on the floor.

4. Once it is in that position, say "Down," give it the treat and generously praise it.

5. Repeat steps 1 through 4 until your dog has it mastered. Repeat every day. If your puppy tries to jump forward or sit up, say "No" and take your hand away. Never push it into the "down" position; that is negative enforcement. Generously encourage every step or movement your puppy makes towards going into the down position, as it is re-programming its natural instincts.

Stay

This is an excellent command to teach your Maltipoo, but don't even begin to teach it to your puppy until it has mastered the "sit" command. This exercise will be teaching your Maltipoo self-control. It is challenging for energetic Maltipoos, but remember that Rome wasn't built in a day either.

1. Tell your dog to "Sit."

2. Open your hand to make a stop sign with the palm of your hand and say, "Stay."

3. Take a few steps backwards. If it stays in the same place, reward it with a treat and lots of praise.

4. Each time you do steps 1 through 3, gradually increase the distance between you and your Maltipoo before you give it the treat.

5. Always give your puppy a treat for staying still, even if it only stayed still for a matter of seconds.

There are many other commands that you can teach your Maltipoo. Since Maltipoos are extremely intelligent, you will find training it to be a relatively easy task.

Should I take my Maltipoo to obedience classes?

❝ *Begin training immediately. Due to their adorable size and personality, many families will not provide a structured environment in the first few critical months (with exercise, discipline and then affection). It is much easier to train a young puppy, than trying to break bad habits of an adult dog."*

Rebecca Posten
riversidepuppies.biz

Obedience classes are highly recommended if you have adopted a rescue or an older Maltipoo, as they will be a little more stubborn at learning new tasks to perform. Puppies are like children, uncoordinated and easily distracted, but with a little orientation they can learn positive behavior.

Many dog owners suggest going to dog obedience school every two or three years to reinforce good behavior that might be getting rusty.

The purpose of obedience school is to teach you to train your dog. There will be no miraculous transformation in your dog from attending obedience school. Practice is the key to having a well-behaved and well-trained dog. Your dog will learn from day-to-day repetition in your house. If you are not taking the time to practice with your dog throughout each day, the sad reality is that you will not have a well-trained dog.

Obedience school will only reinforce the positive training that your Maltipoo is already receiving at home and teach you to train it effectively.

Here are some suggestions to consider before you take your Maltipoo to obedience classes.

- Make sure your Maltipoo's vaccinations are up to date and that it doesn't have any other potential health issues. You don't want to expose your Maltipoo to diseases or put the other dogs at risk.
- Typically, obedience classes for dogs will accept dogs that are older than six months. If you want to enroll your puppy in classes before it is six months old, you can enroll it into puppy kindergarten classes that will teach it how to socialize with other dogs as well as a few basic commands.
- Make sure the instructors only use humane methods for training dogs. Avoid institutions that punish dogs by hitting, scaring, yelling or using electric shocks for bad behavior. You want to look for a system that overlooks bad behavior and rewards good behavior.

- Ask where the trainer was certified to train dogs. You are paying for the classes, so make sure that the teacher didn't learn everything he or she knows online. A certified trainer has met the requirements of the International Association of Canine Professionals (IACP) or Certification Council for Pet Dog Trainers (CCPDT) and has already completed a significant amount of hours training dogs.

- Ask to sit in on a class just to observe before signing your puppy up for the obedience class. This way, you can observe how the trainer treats the dogs and their owners. If he or she treats the owners with respect and care, the same will be true with the dogs.

*Photo Courtesy of
Randi Scanlon*

Teach with love, not fear

The days of punishing your dog for something it is incapable of understanding are over. Many of us grew up with dogs and observed our parents training the household dog, and love normally wasn't one of the ingredients used in obedience training. Many studies have shown that the best way to train a dog is by the use of positive reinforcement.

How can you use positive reinforcement in training your Maltipoo?

Dogs live in the moment, not the past or future, so the best time to praise and reward good behavior is immediately. Rewards can be praise or a treat, given whenever it does something that pleases you.

✔ Do praise and reward your Maltipoo immediately after it does the desired behavior.

Training sessions should be short and fun. Your Maltipoo is very intelligent but it is a puppy and has a short attention span. The goal of each training session should be to leave the class on a positive note, leaving it wanting more.

✔ Do make all training sessions short and sweet.

Treats are treats; they are meant to be something special, exciting and occasional. In the beginning of obedience training, you will need to use quite a few treats to motivate your dog to learn the new behavior. But after it begins to master the new tasks or behavior, the treats should begin to be phased out and replaced with more affection and praise. Maltipoos are companion dogs and aim to please their owners; pleasing you will be their treat.

✔ Do phase out treats and rewards as your Maltipoo begins to master new tasks and replace them with praise and affection.

Avoid making training sessions overly complicated by using key words that are too long, such as saying, "Stay here." Just say "Stay." Dogs respond better to one-syllable words and will be able to remember them more easily. Be specific and simple when teaching your dog. Making the commands and instructions too complicated will just stress your dog out and make it dislike training time.

✘ Don't make training sessions overly complicated.

Avoid being inconsistent with training your Maltipoo. Maltipoos love to have a routine, as they have a fantastic inner clock built into them. Just like children, they need consistency. If you say no to sitting on the couch today but tomorrow you allow it, this will just confuse your Maltipoo and it will not understand what you expect.

It is also important that everyone in your house is on the same page as to how to train your dog. Otherwise, it will go crazy trying figure out what is allowed with who and when.

✔ Do be consistent in training your Maltipoo.

Don't create a spoiled rotten puppy. How can you do that? Bad behavior needs to be corrected. When your Maltipoo acts up and does something inappropriate, don't just let it continue; tell it "No" and redirect its attention to something more productive.

✗ Don't allow your Maltipoo to get away with bad behavior.

A word about physical correction or punishment

Studies have proven that physical correction or punishment is unacceptable and ineffective in training any animal. Why?

Imagine trying to do something while being yelled and screamed at, receiving painful electric shocks for something you don't understand, or being physically hit or kicked. Would you be able to learn something new under this type of stress? Of course not! You would be scared, nervous and very stressed out.

That is exactly how your Maltipoo feels when it is punished; it has no idea why you are mad or what it did wrong. Put yourself in your dog's paws; how would you like to be treated?

Fear inhibits learning. Fear inhibits listening. Fear inhibits trust.

Never, ever use physical punishment to correct your dog's bad behavior.

Not to bark

The Maltese and the Poodle are both known for barking, so it is obvious that your Maltipoo will have inherited the same love for barking from its parents.

Barking in many cases is a habit that appears later on in life. Your Maltipoo might be very quiet as a puppy and even as a young adult, but when it is about two or three years old is when the barking begins. It is typically a behavior that begins later in your Maltipoo's life.

When your Maltipoo begins to bark, it is important to determine the reason behind it. Barking is your Maltipoo's means of communication. If you are unable to understand the reason for its barking, you will not be able to stop it from barking.

Why your Maltipoo might be barking:

- **Fear**: Maybe there was a noise or a something that is out of place and it is frightened. Normally, this will be a fairly loud bark as it is alarmed. This can happen in any location, not just your house.
- **Boredom**: Maltipoo dogs are very social and love human companionship. When they are left alone or ignored for long periods, they will quickly become lonely and bored. Barking is one the less destructive ways they blow off their steam about being left alone. This type of barking can be extremely intense and very passionate on their part. This barking is a guaranteed way to get your neighbors to complain.
- **Stranger danger:** Maltipoo pups become very territorial as they get older, so when someone new approaches them, you, or their house, they will begin to bark. As the threat gets closer, the bark gets louder and louder. When your dog is barking for territorial reasons, it will be quite aggressive and protective.
- **Wanting attention**: Barking is your Maltipoo's way of communicating with you. It will bark to tell you it wants to do go outside, eat, play or get a treat. Normally, you will need to use discernment with this type of barking, as it will look at you, then at the subject of what it wants to do, such as looking at the door to go outside.

How can you teach your Maltipoo not to bark?

All dogs bark, but they can all be taught to be quieter. How can you teach your angelic Maltipoo puppy not to bark?

Boredom: As mentioned above, this is one of the main reasons your Maltipoo might be barking. Maltipoo dogs are bred to be a companion, so they need to be around people. They are not as independent as some other breeds. Maltipoos are known for bonding with their owners and thrive on attention.

If your dog is barking because it is being left alone often, it is lonely and is crying out for you to come home. How can you address this problem?

The problem is your schedule; you are leaving it home too often. You might need to change your behavior before you can change your dog's. Change your schedule so you will be home more often or take it with you to work. Or have a friendly neighbor drop in and check on it every so often, so it doesn't feel so lonely and depressed.

Reminders of what not to do:

Let's imagine your Maltipoo begins to bark. How you react will either encourage more barking or less.

Shouting at your dog to stop barking just gets it even more excited because it will think you are joining in and just bark more. Never yell at your dog to stop barking, just speak calmly and firmly to tell it to be quiet. Your yelling just reinforces the barking.

When your Maltipoo begins to bark, just be patient and ignore it. Wait until it stops barking, then tell it to hush or be quiet. Wait for it to be quiet for twenty to thirty seconds and give it a treat or generously praise it. The key to training your Maltipoo to be quiet with this obedience exercise is the timing. When you reward it for being quiet it will slowly begin to understand that not barking means being rewarded.

Also, you can try distracting your Maltipoo when it begins to bark. Whenever it begins to bark, call your pup over and ask it to do something for you, such as a trick. If you interrupt your Maltipoo's barking, it is less likely to develop the habit of barking.

If you notice that strangers seem to make your Maltipoo bark because it is uneasy, you need to work on helping it to be more comfortable with approaching strangers. How can you do that?

Socialize your Maltipoo as much as possible with other people. Invite friends and family over and introduce them to your Maltipoo. Make sure your Maltipoo feels calm and safe throughout the whole introduction process. If it begins to bark at a person, calm your puppy down and show it that the stranger isn't someone to be afraid of.

Anti-barking collars: The American Society for Prevention of Animal Cruelty states the following: "Anti-barking collars are cruel and not effective." What is an anti-barking collar? It is a collar that has a noise-sensitive device attached to it. When the device is activated by barking, it delivers a small electric shock to your dog (others spray a citrus spray). These collars train dogs not to bark no matter why they are barking and can cause smaller dogs to become fearful and anxious. Also, intelligent dogs such as the Maltipoo quickly discover they are only punished when wearing the collar.

Remember these four suggestions when training your Maltipoo not to bark:

1. Don't react

2. Don't shout

3. Distract your dog

4. Socialize your dog as much as possible with other people

Barking up the wrong tree

Even though you don't speak dog language and your Maltipoo doesn't speak English (or whatever language you speak in your home), you can interpret its desires and intentions, if you know what to listen for in its bark. There are three traits of dog barks that can help you distinguish the reason behind the barking: the pitch, length, and frequency of the bark.

- **Low pitch**: A lower pitch sound such as a growl indicates that a threat is nearby or your dog is upset and angry. Basically, it is saying "Stay away from me or else."
- **High pitch**: A higher pitched sound, like a sharp bark, whine, or a whimper means the opposite of a low pitch; you are allowed to come closer and it is safe to approach. It is a "welcome" bark.
- **Length**: If the dog continues growling (low pitch), that typically means it really doesn't want you to come closer. The length of the sound means it is holding its ground and not backing down. If the growl is in short bursts, it means it is very concerned and fearful, but it isn't sure if it can hold its ground or whether it is totally necessary.
- **Frequency**: There will be barking or whining that is repeated again and again. The closer the sounds are together, the more excitement your Maltipoo wishes to express. If your Maltipoo just gives an occasional bark, it is only slightly interested in something.

Normally, when your Maltipoo feels threatened or in danger the barking will be combined with low-pitched growling. Following is the common interpretation for most barks:

- **Two to four barks in a row**: This is one of the most common forms of barking, which goes back to all dogs' wolf roots. It means "Call the pack." This bark is telling you, the pack leader, that something interesting is happening and it wants you to come see.
- **Barking slowly in a lower pitch but almost non-stop**: Your Maltipoo senses imminent danger. It means "Danger is very close, be prepared to defend yourself."
- **One or two sharp, high-pitched barks**: This is a typical greeting bark, and once your Maltipoo realizes that the stranger is friendly, they will be greeted with this bark. It basically means "Hello there!"
- **A row of barks with a pause in between**: This is a sad bark, which means your Maltipoo feels very lonely and bored. It is your dog's way of asking for some cuddle time and companionship.

- **'Harrruff' or stutter bark:** Normally, this bark is combined with playful body language: your dog's front legs will be flat on the ground and its rear held high in the air. It is ready to play!

As mentioned earlier, your Maltipoo pup might be extremely quiet until it is about two or three years old and then suddenly begin to bark incessantly. Barking is a learned behavior. You will need to practice non-barking training throughout your Maltipoo's lifetime.

Never allow your dog to bark uncontrollably.

Patience is a virtue

66 *Maltipoos are very tender-hearted and do not handle harsh or stern voices or rough handling. They respond wonderfully to praises and love. They are also very fast learners."*

Terry Schulte
valleypuppypaws.com

Obedience training your Maltipoo can be a tedious and frustrating experience. But the key to successfully training your new puppy is having patience. It is necessary to realize you will be teaching this little defenseless puppy a whole new set of commands. You will be potty-training it and teaching it a variety of new behavioral skills.

Imagine you are learning to do ten things at once and your teacher doesn't speak your native language. How would you feel? What quality would you appreciate your teacher showing you? Most likely, most of us would say patience and understanding. This is the same situation your puppy is facing. It wants to do right by you but it doesn't always understand, so please be patient with your little Maltipoo.

In order to be patient with your dog, you need to know its limits. This way you won't require something of it that it is unable to give. Take age into consideration; younger dogs have a short attention span and are easily distracted. It would be wise to keep the training sessions short and sweet for this age group. Adult dogs might be able to learn more complex tasks than puppies. Older dogs might take a little longer in learning to master a new task, but with repetition it can be done.

Maltipoos are eager to please their owners at all ages, but when they are puppies, they tend to get overly excited and think everything is a reason to play. Don't punish your puppy. Remember that it is just being a

Photo Courtesy of
Amy Isett

puppy. You might need to do shorter training sessions throughout the day, until its concentration is better.

Dogs that have a past of being mistreated, abused or physically punished can be more difficult to train. They will need more patience and love than a dog that has come from a loving home, as they will have some trust issues with humans.

Your attitude towards obedience training will play a very important part in how your Maltipoo responds to it. If you are always impatient or quickly become frustrated, then for your own sanity, you will need to do shorter training sessions. You dog can pick up on your negative vibes and begin to imitate them. Also, enrolling in obedience classes will help orient you in how to train your dog, so you don't feel so overwhelmed.

You and your dog both need to be willing to learn, so you need your puppy to bond with you during these training sessions. Your patience, love, and constant praise will make your little Maltipoo respond to you and make it want to please you even more. Obedience training is a long process, so make it enjoyable and fun.

In order for your Maltipoo to understand you, at times you will need to show it exactly what you want. You might have to position your dog for what you want it to do and reward it when it begins to do cooperate, even if it is only halfway done.

Training and rewards

We all love to eat and your Maltipoo is no exception. Treats are a wonderful way to motivate your puppy to learn new things. Treats and rewards go hand in hand with obedience training. It is nearly impossible to train your puppy without motivating it with the occasional treat.

Many of the tasks your want to teach your puppy might be hard for it to comprehend. You will have to use a keyword or sound or even get down on your knees and show your puppy what to do. Even then, your puppy still might not get it. But a treat makes everything easier for it to understand.

How you can use treats in obedience training your Maltipoo

Small treats: Too many treats and rewards are going put stress on your Maltipoo's waistline. It is very easy to overdo it when giving your puppy treats while training it. Try giving it only small treats, or if possible, break the treats into pieces. If you accidentally give your puppy too many biscuits in one day, you could give it less food at mealtime.

When to reward: Never, ever reward bad behavior. By giving a treat you are reinforcing good behavior that you approve of. If your puppy goes into a hyperactive frenzy after doing the command, it will be best not to reward it at that moment.

No bribes here: Reward training is temporary. It is used to motivate dogs in the beginning to learn a new habit and keyword. Over time, there will be more praise and attention than treats for good behavior. You will have to slowly reduce the treats; otherwise your dog will only behave when bribed by a treat.

Reward each baby step: Many dog owners make the mistake of only rewarding their dog once it does the whole task perfectly. This only leads to frustration for you and your puppy. The key to successfully training your Maltipoo is to reward every baby step that it makes towards doing the task. Reward even the slightest progress.

Some days the progress might seem to be backwards, but we all have bad days. So cut your little puppy some slack; it is trying its best to understand what you want. Over time, it will connect the dots and see that the treat is connected to doing a certain task.

Distractions: Puppies can easily be distracted. Make sure the training location you have chosen has no distractions. You want your Maltipoo to concentrate on you and the treat in your hand. Avoid areas where cars are driving by, children are playing nearby, or where there are squirrels.

Something new: Keep your dog excited about the treats you are going to give it. Sometimes the treat you are going to give your puppy just isn't good enough for it to make such a big effort. For the more difficult tasks, choose your pup's favorite treats to motivate it to do the impossible.

Leash training

In a perfect world, dogs would be born knowing how to walk on a leash; but the reality is that you will have to patiently teach your puppy how to walk nicely on a leash. It needs to learn that it is incorrect to pull ahead or lag behind you.

The biggest challenge with training a Maltipoo to walk on a leash is to teach it to walk at your pace. Your puppy is a bundle of energy that wants to do and see everything at once, plus it has an extra set of legs that makes it move a little faster than you might want to.

Why use a leash and collar?

Leashes can constrain your overly curious Maltipoo from getting into trouble such as running into the road and getting hit by a car. Also, Maltipoos have a keen sense of smell and are fascinated by all the smells on their walk. If left to their own devices, they would follow the trail of another dog and most likely end up getting lost.

Also, in most cities, it is required by law to keep your dog on a leash at all times. By having your dog on a leash, you show those around you that you respect them and are a good neighbor. You will be able to clean up after your dog does its dirty deed on the sidewalk or somebody's lawn. A dog wandering about freely will do its dirty deed out of your sight and it will be left for someone else to clean up. Most cities have a fine of up to $5,000 for owners not picking up their animal's excrement.

Collars carry your dog's identification, so if it happens to get lost it will be quickly returned to you.

The local animal control officer will impound dogs that are running at large, or a stranger might decide to claim your dog as his or her own. If your dog is impounded, there will often be an impoundment fee plus a daily fee until you claim your dog. You can avoid this if your Maltipoo is always on its leash.

A leash helps keep the veterinary bills lower. All dogs, no matter how cute they are, love to eat everything they see and smell, garbage included. Also, free roaming dogs can tread through poison oak, pesticides, tick-infested bushes, and plants that have thorns or burrs, or drink contaminated water.

Loose dogs can bite people. Maltipoos pick up on the stress around them and they might accidently bite or scratch someone that becomes frightened of them. If personal injury was caused, legal action could be taken against you and your dog. You might receive a hefty fine and your dog could be euthanized. Keeping your Maltipoo leashed helps you keep your dog safe and under control, and shows that you, the owner, are exercising reasonable precautions.

Having your dog on a leash is just good karma. It shows that you are a good neighbor and that you respect those around you. Not everyone loves dogs as much as you do. Some people might have severe allergies or phobias. Those suffering from phobias or panic attacks might react out of fear and injure your friendly Maltipoo when it runs up to greet them. Using a leash shows that you are in control of your dog and you respect those around you.

A leash is one of the most important items to have for your Maltipoo. It will protect both of you. Since using a leash is beneficial for your dog, those around you, and yourself, how can you train your Maltipoo to use a leash?

How to train your Maltipoo to use a leash and collar or harness:

By following these suggestions you will have your Maltipoo walking on a leash like a pro in no time.

1. **Pick the best leash and collar for your Maltipoo**: Below is a brief introduction to the different types of leashes on the market. When choosing a collar for a new puppy, make sure it is lightweight and thin. You can always change the type of collar later on.

2. **Introduction**: Introduce your puppy to the leash, collar, and harness (if you are using one). Place the leash, collar or harness on it during playtimes. These will be very short periods in the beginning that slowly get longer and longer. Eventually, the collar will stay on permanently. During these short periods of training your Maltipoo to like the leash, give it treats and praise it generously. It will begin to associate the leash and collar with food and fun time.

3. **Practice sessions**: Once it is accustomed to the leash and collar, walk your puppy around the house with it on. Do not try to make it heel right away; the key is letting it understand the boundaries of its leash in the beginning. Walk a few steps with the leash and then stop and give a treat. Continue doing this until your puppy begins to associate following your lead on the leash with getting delicious treats.

4. **Baby steps**: In the beginning, your puppy might try to wiggle its way out of the leash. Just let it be and once it figures out the leash isn't going anywhere, continue walking. Try walking around the house using the three-steps-and-treat method. Small steps will eventually lead to big steps, and you'll be walking around the block.

Types of collars and leashes

It can be overwhelming to choose the correct leash and collar at your local pet supply store. No matter what type of leash you decide to use, remember that the leash is a way of communicating with your Maltipoo. Without using words, you can tell it when to stop, when to go, how fast to walk, etc. Never pull or use excessive force.

Remember, you are the leader of the pack; you are your Maltipoo's hero. Walk straight and take note of your body language. Stand straight, with your head held high and walk like a pack leader, with determination. The energy will be sent to your pup through the leash.

If you have any doubts as to what type of leash and collar to use, consult your veterinarian for some recommendations.

Basic leash and collar: This is the most common leash and collar and is a good fit for most dogs. When using this type of leash and collar, make sure you walk right beside or in front of your dog. This will place you as leader in the pack. Recommended for Maltipoos.

Slip collar: This is a chain that tightens around the dog's neck when you pull or tug on it as a way to correct bad behavior. It isn't recommended for smaller dogs, such as Maltipoos, because it could cause damage to their neck or restrict their breathing. It is mostly used for larger dogs.

Harness: This is a safe option for dogs that have a pushed-in face, such as Pugs, and dogs with long slender necks, like Greyhounds. Harnesses will not restrict breathing or damage the trachea and throat. Recommended for Maltipoos.

Importance of visibility when walking your Maltipoo

Visibility means safety. At nighttime or early in the morning, it can be difficult for drivers to see you walking your dog. You can wear some sort of reflective clothing or a vest, but what about your Maltipoo?

You can purchase a safety harness that has reflective stickers on it. Also, many leashes and collars have added illumination to protect your Maltipoo from an accident. You can purchase reflective tape at your local hardware store and make your own reflective harness and leash for your Maltipoo, if you wish to save money.

CHAPTER SIX
How to care for your Maltipoo

W ho doesn't enjoy a day of getting pampered and spoiled? We all need it every once and a while: a new hair cut, a manicure and pedicure, and maybe even a massage. Sounds wonderful! Taking time for ourselves is one of the best gifts we can give ourselves.

But as the old saying goes, "There's more happiness in giving than receiving." Taking care of your Maltipoo pup will bring you many benefits and much joy.

Your Maltipoo is unable to fend for itself or take care of hardly any of its own basic needs. It needs your help. You need to provide it with shelter, love and food, but it also needs to be groomed and bathed.

Photo Courtesy of
Vicki Mueller

D.I.Y. Grooming

The Maltipoo's parents, the Poodle and Maltese, both require regular grooming and brushing, and your Maltipoo will need the same. It will be necessary to adapt its grooming needs based on the type of hair it inherited:

1. **Straight and Silky**: The dominant genes come from the Maltese when the Maltipoo has a straight and silky coat. This type of coat is not prone to tangling as much as the other two types of coats.
It is recommend to get this type of fur groomed and trimmed every six to eight weeks.
This style of hair allows for a wide variety of hairstyles; it can be left long to look like a typical Maltese, or given the adorable puppy cut.

2. **Thick and curly**: The dominant genes come from the Poodle, which is known for its thick and curly coat of fur. This type of fur is higher maintenance, as it is prone to tangles and mats. It will need regular trims and clipping to prevent it from growing out of control and turning into a huge mess.
If you notice a small tangle or mat forming, quickly try to brush it out or if needed, cut it off. The smallest tangle or mat can quickly turn into a huge one.
It is recommended to have this type of coat groomed and trimmed every four weeks.

3. **Wavy and wiry**: This is a sign of bad breeding practices and is the most undesirable type of coat for a Maltipoo to have. This is the hardest type of fur to maintain, as it quickly forms tangles and mats. The wiry texture makes grooming very troublesome. The only suitable type of haircut for this Maltipoo is to keep it short. It is hard to control so the more stylish haircuts are not recommended.
It is recommend to have this type of coat groomed and trimmed every four weeks.

Here is a brief list of the most popular types of haircuts for Maltipoo dogs; each one is adorable and cute, a perfect complement to their loveable personality:

• **Miami Beach Cut**: This is one of the most popular styles for poodles and is best suited for Maltipoo pups that have thick and curly hair. The face, tail and feet are shaved, leaving a pom-pom shape at the base of feet, top of the head and the end of the tail. The rest of the body is trimmed.

• **Town and Country Cut**: This cut is recommended for all types of Maltipoo coats, but especially looks good on the straight and silky Maltipoo. This is a great haircut for a stylish Maltipoo that loves to play outside. This cut involves shaving the belly, face and legs. The rest of the hair is trimmed and can be left the length you desire and kept up by daily brushing.

- **Kennel Cut**: Also called the military cut. This type of haircut is recommended for all types of Maltipoo coats. The ears are trimmed and brushed out. By using scissors, the groomer will contour the hair on the body; the feet, face and tail are shaved, leaving a pom-pom at the end of the tail.
- **Lamb Cut**: This cut looks adorable on the thick and curly Maltipoo. It is also a popular cut for show poodles. The whole body is trimmed to the same length except for the tail, which has a pom-pom at the end. Adorable!
- **Puppy Cut**: This the most popular cut for all three types of Maltipoo fur. The fur on the whole body is cut close to the body and the hair on the head is brushed and made into a ponytail.
- **Continental Cut**: This haircut is recommended for all Maltipoo hair types. The fur on the entire body is contoured close to the body, except the feet, which have pom-poms at the bottoms.

As you can see, there are a lot of different options for Maltipoo haircuts. If you decide to groom your Maltipoo yourself, it would be wise to get the first haircut done by a professional groomer, then you can just follow the shape when your give your Maltipoo a trim. Whatever hairstyle you choose to give your Maltipoo, it will just be a complement to its loving and sweet personality.

Start early

" *Maltipoos make excellent companions that are very loyal. They are clean and smart which makes them easy to care for and train."*

Renee Banovich
www.aTender1sPuppies.com

The key to grooming any dog is to get it used to the grooming routine early on in its life. As with children, the sooner they learn a good habit or routine, the better.

Even if you are planning on using a professional groomer for your Maltipoo, you still need to train your pup early on for grooming sessions. It will need daily brushing sessions anyway.

Since Maltipooups will need to be groomed regularly for their whole lives, it is important that they are not traumatized by the experience. That is why it so important to get them used to being groomed from day one.

The first day you bring your Maltipoo home, introduce it to the brush. Let it smell and touch the brush, but not play with it or chew on it, as this will teach it that grooming time is play time and not brushing time.

Once the brush has been introduced, begin to lightly brush your puppy. Praise it the whole time that it is sitting still and being good. Only brush for a minute or two and then give a treat for its good behavior. Repeat this process as much as possible the first few days, as it is teaching that the brush is a friend and it means getting treats. With time, it will become a routine.

Make sure all grooming interactions are a positive experience for you and your Maltipoo. If you find yourself dreading teaching your pup how to be groomed, you might need to give yourself a treat too, as a way to motivate yourself. Maybe give yourself a dollar every time you successfully groom your pup.

Also, if you find yourself thinking that grooming your pup is a chore or a burden, that is a warning sign not to groom your pup at that moment. It will pick up your bad vibe towards grooming which will make grooming unpleasant for your puppy. Wait until you are in the right frame of mind to begin grooming to make the experience positive for both you and your Maltipoo.

Longer isn't necessarily better when grooming your Maltipoo; the shorter the training session is, the more productive it is. If you notice your puppy is reluctant to participate, it is a sign to slow down. You might need to use more treats to make the grooming sessions more attractive.

Be prepared from the first day you bring your Maltipoo puppy home to never neglect its regular grooming routine.

Not taking the time to properly teach your Maltipoo pup that grooming is beneficial from day one will lead to deep-rooted bad habits that are almost impossible to break. Since your Maltipoo will be traumatized every time it is groomed, it will be very stressed out. This might lead to it biting or scratching you and making you feel traumatized, causing a lifetime of unhappy grooming sessions. So take the time to teach your puppy that grooming is a fun and bonding time with you from the very first day you bring it home.

Bathing

Most Maltipoo pups love bath time and it is probably one of the most enjoyable grooming tasks. Let us begin with some common questions asked by new Maltipoo owners.

At what age can I begin bathing my Maltipoo?

Once it is more than eight weeks old, it is old enough be bathed. Normally, that is the age of a Maltipoo when it is brought to its new home. But what if you have a puppy younger than eight weeks old? Normally, the mother keeps puppies clean and tidy until they are weaned at the age of four to five weeks. After that, you can just wipe it down with a damp cloth, if necessary.

How often can I give my Maltipoo baths?

It is recommended to bathe your Maltipoo about every three weeks. Bathing a dog too frequently can cause its skin and fur to dry out because it will wash away the natural oils found on the skin. The key is using a good quality shampoo and conditioner designed for the type of hair your Maltipoo pup has.

On the other hand, not washing your Maltipoo enough can make its coat greasy, its hair tangled, its skin pores blocked and even cause it to smell bad.

How to give your Maltipoo a bath

1. **Get yourself ready**: Make sure you are wearing clothes that you don't mind getting wet, dirty and hairy. Gather all the supplies that you will need during bath time so you won't have to run and get something, leaving a wet and soapy puppy alone in the room. Make sure you have on hand shampoo, conditioner, a brush, mineral oil for the eyes, cotton balls or cotton gauze for the ears, two big towels, and most important, lots and lots of treats. If you don't have a detachable showerhead where you are giving the bath, make sure you have a large bowl to help rinse your Maltipoo off.

2. **Fill up the tub or sink with warm water**: This is one of the common mistakes new dog owners make: they put the dog in an empty sink and then begin to fill it up with water. This will only lead to your puppy becoming bored and the bath will be a bad experience.

3. **Get your Maltipoo ready**: Make sure our puppy's nails have been trimmed before beginning to wash it, to avoid accidents. Bring it into the bathroom and shut the door behind you. This will prevent your wet, soapy dog from running around your whole house. Once

in the room, praise your dog generously and give it some treats. Try to make it feel really comfortable in the bathroom before you put it into the tub or sink. If your puppy lets you, put a cotton ball in each ear to prevent water from going in the ear, just don't forget to remove them when finished. If your Maltipoo has sensitive eyes, you can put a drop of mineral oil in each eye, to prevent the shampoo from irritating its eyes.

4. **Bath time**: Make sure you read the directions on the shampoo bottle so you use the right amount of shampoo. Gently place your pup in the tub or sink, making sure the water isn't too hot or too cold. Wet your dog's coat with water before you begin shampooing. Begin shampooing at the shoulders, then move on from there. Be very careful around the mouth and ears. Rinse out all the shampoo, using your fingers to assure all of shampoo has been removed, since that could irritate the skin.

5. **Detangle that fur**: Once you have finished shampooing, you can apply the conditioner. Follow the directions carefully, as some conditioners require sitting for a couple of minutes to soak in. Rinse thoroughly.

6. **Clean the ears**: While the conditioner is soaking into the coat is a good time to wipe your pup's ears clean with the cotton gauze or cotton balls.

7. **Towel drying**: Take your dog out of the sink or tub and quickly wrap it in a towel and try to dry it as quickly as possible. Avoid letting it shake itself until it is almost dry. Brush your dog's coat before you let it exit the room, as baths help all the loose hair fall out. Expect your dog to go crazy and run everywhere once you let it out of the room--that's how it relieves stress.

Drying

As mentioned above, you can towel dry your Maltipoo in the warmer months; but in the colder months it is recommended to use a hairdryer on low. Never point the hairdryer directly at your Maltipoo's face, as that will frighten it and it will not want to be dried with the hair dryer.

If your Maltipoo has inherited the soft, silky Maltese hair, it is recommended to always use the hair dryer, as it tends to become quickly matted and knotted. As you are drying it with the hair dryer, brush its hair upwards, to dry the roots of the hair. This will also help remove any excess hair.

As you are drying, it is best to brush at the same time as all the loose hair from the bath begins to come out. This will keep dog hair from being left throughout your house for you to clean up.

It is important to make sure your Maltipoo is completely dry after a bath because it is prone to catching cold. So don't let your little Maltipoo go outside until it is one hundred percent dry.

Brushing

No matter what type of fur your little Maltipoo has, it will need to be brushed daily. The sooner you get your puppy used to being brushed, the easier it will be when it is older and bigger.

For day-to-day brushing, it is highly recommended to use a pin brush or a slicker brush. These types of brushes are designed for Maltese or Poodle hair textures.

How to brush your Maltipoo's hair:
- Gently sweep the brush through your Maltipoo's hair, being careful not to use too much force and hurt your little angel.
- As you comb through the fur, you will remove the excess hair and prevent future matting.
- If your Maltipoo has inherited the Maltese fine hair, it may be helpful to use a detangling spray designed for dogs when you brush.

How to remove a mat:
- This is a challenge and it can cause your puppy a lot of discomfort. A little mat can grow into a huge mess in a matter of hours, so the key is catching it before it gets too big.
- When you find a mat, first spray it generously with the detangling spray, which will help make it easier to work with. Then, using a brush designed for mats, gently begin to tease the edge of the mat. It will take some time, but you will find that the majority of mats can easily be removed by brushing.
- If you have a stubborn mat that is just too big to brush out, you will need to cut the mat out. Be very careful when cutting the mat because you could snip your puppy's skin. Use your fingers to shield your puppy's skin from the scissors.

If the mat is really large, you might have to cut it into pieces before you can actually remove the mat. You may find that by cutting the mat in half, you can avoid cutting the mat off and instead be able to brush it out. This will help prevent your Maltipoo from having large gaps in its fur.

If you notice that your Maltipoo pup is having a hard time sitting still during a brushing session, the best thing would be to give it some serious playtime so it is tired. Then you can try again, as it will have less energy to try to run away. Forcing your puppy to be brushed when it wants to go will only result in both of you becoming extremely irritated and frustrated.

Ears

Check your Maltipoo's ears weekly, as they are prone to infections.

Maltipoo pups have inherited their droopy ears from both parents. Like humans, dogs have earwax buildup but the Maltipoo's droopy ears make the situation more problematic than with other dog breeds.

Ears are one of the highly sensitive areas for your Maltipoo and many Maltipoo dogs dislike having their ears touched, as they might be ticklish. How can you teach your Maltipoo to let you handle its ears?

Photo Courtesy of
Meredith Edwards

From the first day you bring it home, start handling your puppy's ears. Touch the ears, massage them, and look at the inside while talking to your puppy. Do this every other day. This will help your Maltipoo not to have overly sensitive ears when it is older.

If you have adopted an older Maltipoo that dislikes having its ears touched, try touching the ears each day. Each time, praise it generously and give a treat. Try to touch the ears for a little longer time every day, until it is used to its ears being touched.

How to clean your Maltipoo's ears:
- Flip up your Maltipoo's ears, and check for any sign of infection and any debris, such as grass or dirt. Using a clean, damp cloth, gently wipe the ears clean and remove any earwax.
- Check to see if there are any small cuts or scratches that your Maltipoo may have caused by scratching its ears. If there is a cut, wipe it clean and let it heal on its own.
- If you notice a strong odor proceeding from your Maltipoo's ears, that is a sure-fire sign of infection. You should take your Maltipoo to the veterinarian as soon as possible. Also go to the veterinarian if there is swelling or heat in one spot in the ear.
- Using tweezers, remove any long hairs growing out of the ears, as these can lead to ear infections if not removed.

Nails

Maltipoo toenails grow just like our nails do. How often your Maltipoo's nails will need to be clipped will mostly depend on the type of activity your Maltipoo regularly does. For example, if your Maltipoo regularly walks on pavement, its nails will wear down faster than a dog that walks on grass. The dog that only walks on grass will need its nails clipped more often.

You can cut your dog's nails yourself or you can get your groomer to do it.

How to cut your Maltipoo's nails:

If you decide to cut the nails yourself, you will need to invest in a pair of nail clippers that are designed for small dogs and have some cornstarch on hand.

Make sure your pup is tired and gently hold one of its paws in your hand. Examine the nails closely, and try to identify the nail bed; it will bleed if cut and it will really hurt your puppy.

The nail bed is easy to identify with Maltipoo pups that are lighter in color, as you can see a line of pink in the nail. It is harder to notice in darker colored dogs. Once you have identified the nail bed, you will want to cut about two millimeters below it. Follow the instructions that came with your nail clippers. Most dog nail clippers have to be held in a perpendicular way as opposed to human toenail clippers that have to be held parallel to the nail.

Try to work fast and don't be surprised if your little puppy tries to pull away from you. If it yelps or cries, that means you cut the nail bed. It will soon begin to bleed, so quickly place your Maltipoo's paw into the cornstarch, which will stop the bleeding.

You might not be able to cut more than one paw at each session or maybe even only one nail at a time. There is no rule that says that you need to clip all your Maltipoo's nails in one sitting. You might even opt to do just one a day.

Some dogs don't mind getting their nails cut, but the majority will protest and try to run away.

As mentioned above, from the first day you bring your puppy home, get it used to you holding its paws and touching its nails. With time, your puppy won't have a problem with you holding its paws.

Pedicure time for your Maltipoo

Many Maltipoo owners love to pamper their puppies. They keep them well-groomed and clean cut and most of all, love to put a little bling on their nails. If you decide to paint your Maltipoo's nails with nail polish, here are some simple suggestions to keep in mind.

- Maltipoo pups are curious by nature and love to lick or taste things that are new to them. For this reason, it is not recommended to use human nail polish as it contains chemicals that can be toxic if consumed. Taking into consideration the size of your Maltipoo, the toxicity can be fatal. Only use nail polish that has been designed for dogs.
- Before you apply the doggy nail polish, check your Maltipoo's nails for any cracks or cuts. The nail polish and nail polish remover can hurt your dog's skin.
- After applying the nail polish, carefully watch your Maltipoo. If it is chewing at the nail polish, that means it will be ingested, which will lead to an upset stomach. Normally, when Maltipoo pups are chewing at their nails, it is a sign that they are stressed. Never sacrifice your puppy's health for cosmetic reasons.

Helpful hints in caring for your Maltipoo's nails and paws

Maltipoo pups are indoor dogs but they do enjoy going outside for a brisk walk. During the winter months, however, your little Maltipoo's paws could begin to dry out from the bitter cold outside and the dry heat inside of your house.

How can you protect your dog's paws from becoming cracked and dry?

You can apply a small amount of coconut oil on its tiny paws; this will help prevent the nails and paws from splitting and cracking. Just remember to use a very small amount, as it will try to lick it off. Coconut oil isn't toxic for your Maltipoo, but it does contain unnecessary calories.

By not cutting your dog's nails, you are playing with fire because long, untrimmed nails can easily split, leading to an infection. Also, long nails can be very uncomfortable when walking, causing it to limp, which could lead to posture problems in the future.

The truth is that nobody really enjoys the process of cutting your Maltipoo's nails, neither your pup nor yourself, but it is a very important grooming process that should never be overlooked.

Do-It-Yourself Paw Wax

This is a very simple and cost-effective recipe for making paw wax for your Maltipoo. It contains ingredients that are non-toxic for your dog and will protect it from the harsh chemicals on the ground in the winter or the burning hot cement in the summer. This also makes a great gift for other pet owners.

INGREDIENTS:

- 3 ounces beeswax
- 3 tablespoons coconut oil
- 3 tablespoons avocado oil
- 3 tablespoons calendula oil (if you can't find calendula oil replace with avocado or coconut oil)

INSTRUCTIONS:

1. Stovetop: Put all the ingredients into a pot and melt. Stir occasionally. Pour into a plastic or metal container, let cool 20 minutes and it is ready to use.
2. Microwave: Place all the ingredients in a glass bowl and melt. Stir occasionally. Pour into a plastic or metal container, let cool 20 minutes and it is ready to use

Teeth

> **❝** *Keeping your Maltipoos teeth clean and gums healthy is very important.   You can select from many different types of kibble, but dry kibble is best for their teeth.   Providing toys specifically designed for teeth cleaning is also important."*

Rebecca Posten

riversidepuppies.biz

The good news about your Maltipoo's teeth is that they are not as prone to cavities as your teeth are.

The old wives' tales states that there is nothing cleaner than a dog's mouth. Sadly, this isn't so true. All dogs, including Maltipoos, can develop tartar and plaque buildup, and also gingivitis. Yellow teeth and bad breath aren't the worst of it; your Maltipoo can have the same dental problems you face. These dental problems can lead to infections that can cause heart, liver and kidney disease, and even be fatal. Dental problems can be avoided by practicing simple dog dental care. So how can you take care of your Maltipoo's teeth?

How to train your Maltipoo to let you brush its teeth:

As with any type of dog training, it is vital to begin teaching the new behavior as soon as possible. The longer you wait to get your Maltipoo used to its teeth being brushed, the more likely it will not happen. Your dog will probably become highly agitated when you touch its mouth and you will be afraid to try.

Start training your Maltipoo for dental hygiene while it is still a puppy, when it will be more adaptable and easygoing about you touching its teeth.

Let your Maltipoo taste the toothpaste for the first few days. Place a very small amount on your fingertip and let your dog lick it off. If you find it isn't too keen on the flavor, switch to another flavor. Use a special toothpaste designed for dogs. Human toothpaste contains fluoride, which is extremely toxic for dogs and can cause kidney failure leading to death. Never, ever use your toothpaste to clean your dog's teeth.

From the first day that you bring your Maltipoo home, begin rubbing your fingers over its gums and teeth. Do this daily until you begin to actually brush its teeth. It will help your dog become accustomed to its teeth being touched, making cleaning its teeth easier in the future.

Once it is used to you regularly touching its gums and teeth, introduce the toothbrush. Maybe just brush two teeth at a time, until it is more comfortable with the procedure.

The first couple times you brush your dog's teeth, light bleeding might occur. Slight bleeding is okay, but heavy bleeding that continues after brushing is either a sign that you have been brushing too aggressively or a warning sign of gum disease. See your veterinarian for advice.

How to brush your Maltipoo's teeth:

1. **Pick the right moment**: The best time to brush your Maltipoo's teeth is when it is relaxed and calm. The goal is to set up a daily routine for brushing its teeth, if possible. If it has a healthy mouth, you could brush its teeth three times a week. Pick a schedule and stick to it.

2. **Have your tools on hand**: Make sure you have toothpaste designed for dogs; one of the most popular flavors is peanut butter. Use a soft-bristled toothbrush designed for small dogs or you can opt for the finger brush. Be sure to have a treat ready to give your puppy as a reward for good behavior. Have the toothpaste already on the toothbrush.

3. **Right position**: You both need to be comfortable. Avoid standing above your Maltipoo or forcefully holding it down; this will make your Maltipoo feel threatened. Kneel down beside your Maltipoo or place it at your level. Make sure your Maltipoo doesn't feel threatened. It should be in a sitting position and you should be at the same level it is.

4. **Check the gums**: Using light pressure, lightly rub your clean fingers along the gums. This gets them prepared for the toothbrush. This will also help you see if there are any wounds or broken teeth.

5. **Brush time**: Lift up the upper lip; hold the toothbrush at a 45-degree angle, touching where the gums and teeth meet. Move the toothbrush in a circular motion, removing any plaque or tartar that has formed. Focus on the back teeth, as that is where plaque tends to build up. Aim to brush the teeth for about two minutes maximum.

6. **Reassure your pup**: The whole time you are brushing, talk in a reassuring voice, praising your Maltipoo for being such a good dog. This will keep it relaxed and at ease.

7. **Reward time**: Once you have finished brushing, it is time to reward your dog with its favorite treat and some special playtime with you.

Warning signs that your Maltipoo has dental problems:

Look at your dog's mouth weekly, and if you notice any of the following symptoms, take your Maltipoo to the veterinarian as soon as possible.

- Bad breath (not just dog breath)
- A change in your dog's chewing or eating habits
- Pawing at its mouth or face
- Depression, not wanting to eat or play
- Excessive drooling
- Missing teeth (after the teething period)
- Discolored or broken teeth
- Red, swollen gums or bleeding gums
- Growths or bumps inside of the mouth
- A yellowish-brown tartar buildup near the gum line

How does dental disease affect your Maltipoo?

The dental tartar or plaque that slowly builds up on your dog's teeth is made up of about eighty percent bacteria, which damages the gums, the bone beneath the gums and the ligaments that are holding the teeth in place. Once this has access to the blood stream, it begins to infect the heart, lungs and kidneys. Advanced dental disease is very painful for your dog and for your wallet. The only way to prevent dental disease is by regularly brushing.

How often should the veterinarian check my Maltipoo's teeth?

We need to get our teeth professionally checked every six months to a year. Just like us, our dog needs to have its teeth checked every six to twelve months.

Your veterinarian can look at them when your Maltipoo is having its annual check-up. Just make sure when you make the appointment that the veterinarian has enough time to do a dental hygiene check.

Providing your dog with dental hygiene does seem like a pain, but proper dental maintenance can be a big money saver in the future. Not cleaning your Maltipoo's teeth can lead to costly and often very painful veterinarian visits in the near future. Many times, your dog will have to be given anesthesia to have its teeth and gums cleaned if there is a bad tartar buildup.

Take the time now to keep your dog's mouth clean and you will both have something to smile about in the future.

How to strengthen your Maltipoo's teeth:

One way to clean your dog's teeth is by giving it crunchy food. Soft food is more likely to get stuck in the teeth and cause decay. Crunchy dry dog food helps to clean the teeth.

Also, there are many chew toys on the market that are specifically designed to strengthen your dog's teeth and gums. You can find them at your local pet supply store. Avoid choosing chew toys that are hard, as they could lead to a broken tooth that could cause an infection.

Also, all dogs love to chew on bones. Chewing on a bone will help keep off the tartar build-up and strengthen teeth.

These suggestions are not meant to replace regularly cleaning your dog's teeth but to help promote good dental hygiene. Would you chew gum and use mouthwash but not clean your teeth? No, you know that the best way to clean your teeth is with a toothbrush and toothpaste. The same goes for your little Maltipoo puppy. Dry dog food, chew toys and bones are not enough.

Retained baby (primary) teeth:

Small dogs like Maltipoos often will not lose their puppy or baby teeth because of their small jaw. They will need to be pulled out by a licensed veterinarian to allow the adult teeth to grow in. Often this is done when your puppy is being neutered or spayed.

If the puppy teeth aren't removed, it will cause overcrowding in an already small jaw and the adult teeth won't be able to grow in straight. Crooked and uneven teeth cause food to become stuck in them and plaque to build up. This plaque buildup results in bacterial growth, causing smelly breath and gum and dental disease.

Periodontal disease:

This is canine gum disease caused by plaque buildup on the teeth. Over 80 percent of all dogs suffer from this condition because their owners did not look after their dog's teeth. This disease can be completely avoided by regularly cleaning your dog's teeth.

It is a painful disease causing your Maltipoo to become miserable. It can make eating painful and some of the bacteria might infect the heart, liver and brain.

If you notice that your Maltipoo begins to have bad breath, that could a sign of gum disease caused by plaque buildup on its teeth.

Secondly, if you notice that your Maltipoo is excessively drooling, it might be suffering from gum disease. It might be experiencing pain or its salivary glands could be sore and inflamed from the bacteria in its mouth. It would be wise to call your veterinarian and set up an appointment.

Tools needed for grooming

Here is a basic list of supplies you will need for grooming your Maltipoo. Whether all of the supplies are necessary will depend on whether you will be using a professional groomer or doing it yourself.

These are suggestions to help you get started, but it isn't necessary to run out and purchase all of these items before you bring your Maltipoo home for the first time. You can acquire additional items over time, as you need them.

Equipment needed for grooming your Maltipoo

- **Bristle brush**: This type of brush will remove any loose hair, dirt or debris. It will stimulate your Maltipoo's skin, improve its circulation and add a shine to its coat. Be gentle to avoid injuring your dog.

- **Pin brush**: This is similar to the bristle brush, but has more widely spaced bristles with a rubber coating on the tips for gentler brushing. Groomers normally use this brush after the bristle brush, to fluff up the dog's hair.

- **Slicker brush**: This brush has short wire bristles, packed closely together on a rectangular surface. This is an ideal tool for removing mats and tangles from your Maltipoo's hair. Groomers also use them to make the dog's coat look smooth and shiny.

- **Mat splitters**: The name explains the purpose of this brush. Mat splitters come in three different styles: letter opener style, safety razor style and a curved blade style. These tools are used to split matted fur into smaller pieces without causing your puppy too much discomfort.

- **Combs**: Combs are extremely useful in removing mats since they can get down to the root of the mat or tangle and slowly loosen it up. Some combs have rotating teeth, which makes removing the tangles much easier with no need to pull your Maltipoo's fur.

- **Flea comb**: Again, the name describes the purpose of this comb. It is designed for removing fleas from your dog's coat. The flea comb is very small, so it can fit into spaces that are hard to reach, such as behind the ears, in the armpits, etc.

- **Scissors**: It is recommended to invest in a pair of high quality scissors, to trim around eyes between grooming sessions or to remove a troublesome mat that just doesn't want to be brushed out.
- **Shampoo and conditioner**: Make sure the brand you choose has been designed for canines and for the type of fur your Maltipoo has. Follow the instructions on the bottle.
- **Two washcloths**: You'll need one for washing your dog and the other for covering your dog's eyes during rinse time.
- **Two big towels**: Used for drying your puppy off after the bath
- **Sterile gauze pads**: Used for cleaning the ears.
- **Tweezers**: Used to pluck any hair growing out of the ears.
- **Leave-in conditioner**: To prevent mats and tangles, this can be sprayed on the fur after grooming. Follow the instructions on the bottle.
- **Toothbrush and toothpaste**: You can purchase a toothpaste and toothbrush designed for dogs at your local pet supply store. You might need to experiment with different flavors of toothpaste until you find the one that your Maltipoo tolerates.
- **Nail clippers**: These come in all shapes and sizes, but you will want to choose one that is designed for smaller dogs.
- **Paw wax**: This can be purchased at your local pet store; it is used to protect your Maltipoo's paws when outside during the bitter cold winter months and the burning hot summer months.

Going to the groomer

Maltipoo puppies are the offspring of two dog breeds with fur that requires special care and attention. Poodles have curly, thick fur and Maltese have fur that is sleek and fine. Both breeds require professional grooming, so it is reasonable to expect that the Maltipoo will need to be professionally groomed too.

First impressions last

You want your Maltipoo's first impression of the groomer to be a positive one. You should try to find a groomer that comes highly recommended and make sure he or she is willing to groom your puppy, since some groomers only accept certain breeds.

How can you make your puppy's first visit to the groomer positive?

Set up a meet-and-greet appointment with your groomer a few days before the actual grooming. The groomer can meet your Maltipoo and play with it for a few minutes. Bring some of your pup's favorite treats for the groomer to give to your puppy.

While they are greeting each other, try to slip away for a few minutes. This will help your puppy understand that you are coming back and you aren't abandoning it with this strange person.

Having a meet-and-greet with the groomer will break the ice for the actual grooming date. When you go back for the appointment, your puppy will associate the groomer with something positive--getting treats and being petted. This will make it less traumatic for both you and your puppy when you leave it with the groomer for the first time.

When making the appointment to meet the groomer for the first time, make sure it is at a time when there are no other dogs on the premises. This might intimidate your little Maltipoo, causing it to be stressed and upset.

When should my Maltipoo puppy go to the groomer for the first time?

Photo Courtesy of
Amanda Hazy

Around four months old is the recommended age to start going to the groomer. Before this point, your little puppy is just too hyper to sit still and let its fur be clipped. Most professional groomers will not accept a puppy younger than four months, as they know the chances of accidently snipping the puppy are greater.

Is it really necessary to groom my Maltipoo pup?

What will happen to your Maltipoo's fur if you don't get it trimmed regularly?

The same thing that would happen to human hair--it will develop split ends. This will lead to increased shedding, which will mean more work for you cleaning up dog hair around your house and on your clothes. Split ends can also weaken the hair follicles, making the fur more prone to matting, meaning more work for you with brushing and cutting out the endless mats that appear each day.

When Maltipoo pups are not well-groomed, they will quickly form more mats upon more mats. The skin underneath those mats becomes red and inflamed, because the fur is tugging and pulling on it. If mats are not cut off in time, the inflamed skin can become infected, leading to more health problems.

So in the long run, having your Maltipoo professionally groomed will save you a lot of time and energy. Plus, regular grooming is an essential part of your Maltipoo's health. Professional grooming isn't just a cosmetic procedure.

What kind of haircut should my Maltipoo have?

A good groomer will look at your Maltipoo and tell you what kind of haircut is suited for the type of fur your Maltipoo has. There are no standard cuts for a Maltipoo, but generally speaking, the shorter the haircut, and the easier it is to maintain and keep up. A common hair cut for a Maltipoo is the puppy or lion cut, where all of the fur on the body is cut quite short but left longer on the head, feet and tail. It is adorable!

Before choosing a specific cut, be sure to ask your groomer these questions:

1. How can I maintain this cut daily?

2. How can I keep my dog looking in top shape?

3. When should it come back for a trim and a wash?

When making an appointment, ask if bathing and nail trimming are included in the price.

Is it really necessary to use a professional groomer?

It might be tempting to save some money, but really, paying a professional groomer is worth every penny. Why? It is a job that involves a lot of skill, training and special equipment.

Would you let just anyone cut your hair or give you a manicure? Of course not! They might make you look hideous and foolish, or hurt you while cutting your nails because they haven't been properly trained.

The same goes for your puppy. You could groom it yourself, but you risk giving it a silly looking haircut or even injuring your pup. Your Maltipoo doesn't understand the need to sit still for a haircut, so it is extremely complicated to clip its hair. Grooming is best left to your professional groomer.

Hints your groomer wishes you knew:

These seven tips will benefit the physical and emotional wellbeing of your Maltipoo and make your groomer's job more enjoyable.

1. **Prepare your dog**: From the day you bring your puppy home, get it used to being touched in sensitive or ticklish areas such as the feet, ears, and under the legs (armpit).

   It is every groomer's nightmare to have to cut a dog's nails when it is skittish and upset if it can't stand its paws being touched. Make sure your puppy is used to being touched. Your groomer doesn't want to put the muzzle on your Maltipoo puppy, but he or she might have to, if your puppy tries to bite every time it gets touched.

2. **Start grooming as early as possible**: Puppies are more adaptable than older dogs. That is why groomers wish all puppy parents would start grooming their puppies by four months old. Also, the earlier you start, the less matted its hair will get.

   The older the dog, the more traumatic the experience will be. Never fall into the trap of thinking that your puppy doesn't need to be groomed yet. The longer you put it off, the more your puppy and the groomer will suffer.

3. **Brush regularly:** Your Maltipoo's hair is like your hair. If you don't brush your hair for a couple of days it will look messy and become tangled and matted. The same goes for your Maltipoo. The less you brush its fur, the harder those knots and mats will be to remove.

   Also, brushing your puppy regularly helps it not to be overly sensitive in certain areas, since it is used to being touched. This will help it not be nervous and upset during grooming sessions.

   As mentioned before, matting can be a serious problem, causing your Maltipoo's skin to become irritated. Mats that aren't taken care of can become far more difficult to remove, and in those cases, your groomer will just have to shave off the fur.

4. **Please give clear instructions:** Groomers can't read your mind and they work with several dogs each day, so be clear and specific as to what you want done. If you want a certain haircut, please bring in a picture to show your groomer. If you just want the nails trimmed and a quick clip, please let the groomer know. Communication is the key to the experience being positive for all three of you.

5. **Listen to your groomer's suggestions:** They have received professional training on how to groom your dog. This means they will have a general idea of what kind of cut will look good on your dog and what will look horrible. If your groomer suggests something differ-

ent than what you wanted, listen to the suggestions and sincerely consider them.

6. **Keep calm and don't stay and watch:** When you drop off your puppy at the groomer, be calm and relaxed as your pet can pick up on both your negative and positive vibes. If you are stressed about leaving your little munchkin at the groomer, chances are it will be stressed too, leading to an uncomfortable experience for both your dog and the groomer.

By the way, don't drop by to see if your pet is finished or just to watch. Your puppy will hear your voice and get excited, making grooming almost impossible.

7. **Wash away:** Many pet owners are afraid that if they bathe their Maltipoo too often it will dry out their dog's skin. This isn't a problem if you choose the correct shampoo. If you are unsure what type of shampoo to use, ask your groomer for a recommendation.

Frequent washing makes your groomer's job easier and will help prevent future skin problems.

Anal Glands

Anal glands, also called anal sacs, are two small pockets that are located on either side of the anus at four and eight o'clock. These sacs empty through a tiny duct into the anus. Each sac is filled with sebaceous oil glands and lots of sweat glands. When the combined secreted substance is released, it is a brownish fluid that has a dreadful odor.

Dogs mark their territory and identify each other by using this smelly substance produced in their anal glands. This is why dogs often sniff at each other's behinds. It also serves as a lubricant to help their poop come out smoothly.

When you are grooming your Maltipoo you will have to check its anal glands. If you are getting it professionally groomed, ask the vet to check and make sure the glands are not impacted.

Small dogs such as Maltipoos are prone to anal gland disease, especially if they are a little overweight. Normally, when a dog poops, the fluid in the anal sacs is pushed out; the problem begins when the sacs are not completely emptied. The fluid left behind in the sacs becomes dry and thick, which causes the opening to plug up and become impacted.

How can you tell if the anal glands are impacted?

These are four common signs of an impacted anal gland:

- Bad smell coming from its rear end
- Scooting
- Constipation or pain when pooping or sitting
- Trying to lick or bite its rear end

How can you take care of the anal sacs?

They are very easy to care for. By gently squeezing near the anus, you can empty the sacs. It's a good idea to do this before giving your dog its bath every three weeks, so you can wash away the stinky smell.

1. **Suit up**: Wear old clothes and if you find the smell unbearable, put a clothespin on your nose. You can wear disposable latex gloves, if desired.

2. **Paper towels**: Fold up several paper towels to absorb the nasty substance.

3. **Position your dog**: Looking at your Maltipoo's rear-end, with one hand lift up the tail and hold the paper towel as close to the anus as possible.

4. **Squeezing**: Use your thumb and forefinger to very gently squeeze at the four and eight o'clock positions, just below the anus. Make sure your face is out of the way, as it is common for the liquid to squirt out of there.

5. **Clean up**: Throw the paper towels away and wash your Maltipoo's rear end. Once again, it is preferable to empty the anal sacs just before bath time.

Note: When squeezing the anal sac, if you notice that no fluid comes out, your Maltipoo might have an impacted sac, which means it will need to see the veterinarian soon.

If you find your dog is often having impacted anal sacs, you might need to add more fiber to its diet. This will increase the size of its poop, which will put more pressure on anal sacs and easily push out the fluid.

When left untreated, the anal sacs can become infected. If you notice yellow fluid or blood oozing out of the sacs, take your Maltipoo to your veterinarian. Your vet will have to clean the sacs out, which will be very painful for your pup, and give it antibiotics for a few days.

An infection that is left untreated turns into an abscess full of pus; this is extremely painful for your Maltipoo. This abscess could break open at any time. Your veterinarian will have to open the abscess and clean it out. The vet will prescribe antibiotics and anti-inflammatory medicine to help the swelling go down.

If your Maltipoo keeps have problems with impacted anal glands, your veterinarian might recommend surgically removing the anal sacs.

It is a simple operation, but many times, it has side effects such as fecal incontinence, where the poop leaks out uncontrollably.

How can you prevent your Maltipoo from having impacted anal sacs?
- Healthy diet, with plenty of fiber
- Lots of exercise
- Regular check-ups at the veterinarian to check the anal sacs
- Not overfeeding your Maltipoo; the more overweight it is, the bigger the chance of having impacted anal sacs.

What if your dog won't let you touch its rear end?

This is a common problem, as the anal area is extremely sensitive.

The best way for your dog to get used to being touched in this area is to begin to get it used to it from the very first day your bring your puppy home. Puppies are more adaptable, and this will help prevent the area from becoming overly sensitive.

If you find you just don't have the stomach to clean out your dog's anal glands, you can ask your groomer or veterinarian to do it for you at a nominal fee.

Tearstains

Watery eyes cause tear staining, a common condition with smaller dogs. The Maltese breed especially suffers from tearstains, so it is natural for your little Maltipoo to have the same problem. Tearstains leave the fur around the eyes constantly wet, causing it to become stained.

Sometimes the tearstains can even spread to around the Maltipoo's mouth and paws, but that is an extreme case of tear staining. Tearstains will leave a reddish rusty color around the eyes. Tearstains can be caused by a number of different factors, including minerals found in the drinking water, a yeast infection, or something irritating the eyes. It could also be allergies, poor food quality, or blocked tear ducts.

Drinking water: Many owners of professional Maltese show dogs only give their dogs distilled or bottled water to drink. Most of the tap water we drink is packed with minerals that irritate your dog, causing it to cry.

Your Maltipoo's water could even become contaminated right in its drinking bowl.

Have you ever noticed a slimy build-up that is under the water's surface? This slime is called biofilm, which is basically different bacteria that have bonded together into the slimy substance that adheres to the surface of your dog's water dish. This slimy substance is a mixture of bad and good bacteria.

Can these bacteria make your dog sick?

Yes, they can upset your Maltipoo's system, causing it to have tearstains or watery eyes.

It can also cause tummy upset and diarrhea. It can potentially make you sick as well, when you pick up the dirty water bowl and refill it without even thinking. The best way to prevent your Maltipoo's water dish from developing biofilm is to wash the water dish daily.

How to clean your dog's dishes:
1. Wash dishes with hot soapy water daily.
2. Use a dishcloth that is designated solely for your dog's dishes.
3. If you have a dishwasher, put them through the cycle at least once a week to kill off any unwanted bacteria. This will disinfect the bowls.

How to disinfect your pup's dishes without a dishwasher:

One option:
Soak the dishes in mixture of two parts water to one part bleach for approximately ten minutes. Rinse thoroughly with water.

Second option:
Using the same amounts of water, baking soda, and salt, mix together to form a paste. Use the paste to scrub the bowls. Rinse thoroughly with water.

The best types of water and food dishes are made from stainless steel or ceramic. Plastic bowls contain dyes that can irritate your Maltipoo. Many Maltese and Maltipoo owners have stated that their pups' tear stains were a bright red color, which was caused by their red water dish. The best advice is to avoid using plastic dishes.

Yeast infections

There is a very minor chance that your Maltipoo's tearstains are being caused by a yeast infection in these areas. It is red yeast and is harmless. A round of antibiotics will clear it up in no time. Some veterinarians don't consider tearstains to be a serious enough issue to address, but if you are concerned about it, find a new veterinarian that is willing to hear your concerns.

Eye irritation

Many times, there is a piece of fur or eyelash that is pointing into the eye and is irritating the sensitive tissue around the eye, causing it to water. Take a close look at your Maltipoo's eyes to ensure that nothing is inside them.

Make sure to regularly trim around your pup's eyes; this will help prevent tears and watery eyes. Also, longer hair is more likely to trap bacteria and yeast, which leads to eye irritation.

How can you remove your Maltipoo's tearstains?

You can make a simple lightening paste that can be applied daily until the stains disappear.

Combine one tablespoon of Milk of Magnesia, one tablespoon of hydrogen peroxide, and one tablespoon of cornstarch; mix together until a thick paste is formed. You might need to add more starch. Carefully apply underneath your Maltipoo's eyes, avoiding letting it get into the eyes. Using a fine comb or an eyelash brush, brush the mixture away from the eyes, across the tearstained areas. Let it sit for several hours, or even better, overnight. Remove the mixture with a damp cloth. Apply on a daily basis until the stains have faded.

It is also possible to purchase tearstain remover at most pet supply stores.

A simple homemade solution that will change the pH level of your dog's tears and prevent tearstains is to add a teaspoon of organic apple cider vinegar to your dog's water daily. The higher the alkalinity in your dog's tears, the less chance bacteria and yeast have to grow.

Before you remove the tearstain, it is recommended to ask your veterinarian if there are any health conditions causing the tearstains. Some tearstains are caused by injury, infection, ingrown eyelashes, or foreign objects embedded in the eye.

Exercise

All living creatures have a need for exercise. Even though your Maltipoo will be spending most of its time inside your house, it still needs both indoor and outdoor exercise to keep healthy.

Exercise keeps your dog's blood flowing, muscles in good shape, and its little heart going strong. Plus, it will have a healthy appetite, sleep better at night, and keep its weight down.

Exercise also promotes good behavior. Studies have proven that when a dog gets enough exercise, behavioral issues almost disappear. Regular walks around the block help your Maltipoo blow off all the extra energy it has; otherwise that energy would be used in a negative way.

Outside exercise

" *Maltipoos do not need the extensive exercise that larger or 'work' dogs do. They love walks and traveling, but can do with running around your back yard."*

Terry Schulte
valleypuppypaws.com

Your Maltipoo is going to love being outside in the fresh air and playing in the grass. Just remember to use caution when meeting other dogs until your Maltipoo has received all of its shots.

Many people think that small dogs such as Maltipoos don't need exercise, but no matter their size, dogs need exercise. They won't need as much exercise as a bigger dog or be able to run long distances, but they will need some form of daily activity, no matter their age.

Since your Maltipoo is so small, some precautions should be taken before taking your little baby outside. The biggest factors to consider are cold and hot weather.

Cold weather: Maltipoos can get chilled very fast. On colder days, make sure you put a sweater on your Maltipoo to protect it from the cold. This is even more important if your Maltipoo's fur is the straight and silky type. If the weather outside is below thirty-two degrees Fahrenheit or zero degrees Celsius, be sure to limit your time outdoors to twenty minutes at a time.

Maltipoo dogs love to play in the snow, but never let them play in the snow unsupervised.

In snowy areas, a chemical is used on the sidewalks and roads that melts the ice. This substance can cause damage to your Maltipoo's paws.

For this reason, it is recommended that during the snowy season, you put waterproof booties on your dog's paws. Or you can purchase or make some paw wax to protect your best friend's little paws.

Hot weather: Maltipoo dogs have a hard time in extreme heat. For temperatures above eighty-five degrees Fahrenheit or thirty degrees Celsius, it would be wise to limit your Maltipoo's time outdoors to twenty minutes at a time. Try walking your dog earlier and later in the day, when the temperatures are more reasonable.

Maltipoo dogs are prone to becoming overheated and that can lead to a serious condition of heat exhaustion or heat stroke.

When your Maltipoo is outside at the temperatures mentioned above, be sure to bring some water for it to drink along the way. At your local pet supply store, you can buy a collapsible water bowl that is easy to carry along with you.

Hot surfaces and pavement might not seem hot to you, but you are wearing shoes. For your Maltipoo, it is like walking on burning coals. Walking on hot surfaces can actually burn your puppy's paws. It is recommended to put little booties on your Maltipoo or use paw wax to protect its little paws.

How much exercise does your Maltipoo need?

Maltipoos need at least thirty minutes of exercise a day. It is recommended to give your Maltipoo two twenty-minute walks per day.

Exercise doesn't just mean walks. It can be playing catch, hide-and-seek, or any cardio activity. Keeping your Maltipoo active helps it burn off extra energy that could result in misbehavior such as barking or chewing on your furniture.

Can I overwalk my Maltipoo?

This depends on the type and duration of walk. Normally, Maltipoos can be walked a few times a day, for up to thirty minutes. But their strides are tiny compared to ours. A thousand steps for us will be many thousands of steps for them, so they can get tuckered out pretty fast. Vigorous forms of exercise like running long distances or climbing hills are not recommended for your Maltipoo.

When is the best time to take my Maltipoo for a walk?

All dogs love to have a regular schedule, especially Maltipoos. They have a wonderful internal clock, which helps them remember precisely when it is time to eat, go to the bathroom, sleep or play. They get very disappointed when exercise or playtime is cancelled.

You can decide the schedule that works best for taking your little Maltipoo outside for a stroll. Many pet owners find one walk in the morning and another after dinner works best for them. Try to avoid walking your Maltipoo too close to bedtime, as it will be very excited and have a difficult time going to bed.

Indoor games that your Maltipoo will love

There will be days that being outside longer than five minutes will be almost unbearable because of the freezing cold. But you can still burn off your Maltipoo's excess energy by playing games inside your house. One game every Maltipoo just adores is Hide-and-Seek; they could play this game for hours. How can you play Hide-and-Seek with your dog?

Many Maltipoo dogs will just play Hide-and-Seek with you, no toys needed. But other dogs need to see a toy to begin playing. When playing with a toy, make sure your puppy sees where you hid it, maybe under the couch or a small pillow on the floor. Then act like you are looking for it too; your Maltipoo, being very intelligent, will find it for you. Then generously praise it. Once it has mastered this part of the game, you can make it more challenging: make your dog sit far away while you hide the toy, or show it to your dog, then hide it in the other room, and ask the dog to find it.

Another favorite game is playing with an ice cube on the kitchen floor. This will fascinate your puppy until it has totally melted. This is a great game during the hot summer months and for teething puppies.

Whatever games you decide to play with your Maltipoo puppy, inside or outside, make sure it doesn't have to jump up or down, as Maltipoos are prone to slipped kneecaps and dislocated hip joints.

CHAPTER SEVEN
Maltipoo dietary needs

Maltipoos are high-energy dogs that love to eat. Growing up, it was common to hear our parents tell us, "You are what you eat." Maybe you have even said it to your own children. The meaning of this saying is, "If you eat healthy foods you'll be healthy and if you eat unhealthy foods you'll be unhealthy." It is a basic truth that can't be denied.

Every cell in our body is formed by the food we consume, what we drink and by the air we breathe. Literally, we are what we eat. The food we eat affects how we feel, our appearance, our overall wellbeing, our health, mood and weight. Many of us see the importance of eating whole foods and avoiding processed foods.

Your Maltipoo eats whatever you give it. It is made up of that food. Maybe you just pick up a bag of dry dog food at the supermarket, without giving it a second thought. But is it really healthy? Are you helping your pet to be healthy or unhealthy?

How you feed your Maltipoo will have a direct effect on its future, on its physical health. From the first day you brought your Maltipoo home, you made a commitment to give it the best life possible. But how can you take care of its nutritional needs correctly?

In this chapter, we will discuss how much and what to feed your Maltipoo.

Daily nutritional needs

Humans and dogs both need basic nutrients to survive. Dogs need water, protein, carbohydrates, minerals and vitamins.

Maltipoo puppies have a faster metabolism than adult Maltipoos so their nutritional needs differ slightly. Puppies will need to eat more often throughout the day because their tummies are so small and can't hold much food.

During the first two years of your Maltipoo's growth, it is important for it to receive the proper nutrients that ensure bone growth. During this time period, your Maltipoo is growing extremely fast and is burning more calories than an older dog. This is why it is so important for it to receive the correct amount of nutrients, minerals and vitamins needed to grow in a healthy way.

Human dietary needs change during different stages of our lives, depending on our age and other factors. Dogs' dietary needs also change according to the stage of their lives.

The food you feed your dog must include:

1. Energy that comes from carbohydrates
2. Protein
3. Fats, including fatty acids
4. Vitamins, minerals and micro-nutrients

Photo Courtesy of
Andrea Malachowski

How much and when

" *Maltipoos can have sensitive stomachs. You will want to avoid table food as much as possible. Feed a good quality all natural dry food."*

Renee Banovich
www.aTender1sPuppies.com

If it were up to most dogs, they would be eating non-stop for twenty-four hours a day, seven days a week. Seconds after devouring their own meal, they can be drooling at the thought of eating their owners' meal. Most dogs love to eat and eat, and your Maltipoo is no exception.

Maltipoos can suffer many of the same ailments we face from overeating. Overfeeding your Maltipoo can cause it to gain weight and even become obese, which brings a truckload of other health problems, such as diabetes and heart failure.

The amount your Maltipoo needs to eat every day will depend on its size, age and build, metabolism and activity level. Each Maltipoo is unique, just like people, and they don't all require the same amount of food.

A Maltipoo that is extremely active will need more calories than a couch potato Maltipoo. Also, the type of food needs to be taken into consideration. The higher quality the food, the less food needed; the poorer quality the food, the more food needed.

Avoid leaving your Maltipoo's dish constantly full, as that is a guaranteed way to have an obese dog.

How can you tell if your Maltipoo is overweight?

Look it over, first seeing if you can locate its waistline. It shouldn't look like a wide log; its shoulders should be wider and then narrow down towards its waist and hips. Next, place your hands on its back with your thumbs along its spine, and with your fingers try to feel its ribcage. You should be able to feel the ribs without pressing too hard. If you can't, it is time for a diet and more exercise.

Never ever feed your Maltipoo from the table, as this teaches it bad behavior and encourages it to beg and overeat. Make sure everyone in your family follows this rule.

How often should you feed your Maltipoo?

It is recommended to feed adult dogs twice daily, once in the morning and once in the evening, around your dinnertime. This helps you to monitor your dog's daily intake and to keep its routine in sync with yours. This also helps to keep it regular.

Puppies should have several small meals a day until they are potty trained, and then it is recommended to feed them three to four times a day until they are nine months old, as their metabolism is working overtime and they need more calories.

Make sure your dog has access to fresh water all day, every day.

How much should you feed your Maltipoo?

Your dog's age and activity level will determine how much it should eat daily.

Most dog food bags have a table on the back of bag explaining the correct portion to feed your dog according to its weight and activity level. Be sure to check before giving your Maltipoo its meal. The chart below will give you a basic idea of the amount of food a small dog should receive daily. The amount might differ according to your Maltipoo's age, metabolism and activity level. Don't forget to divide the amount in half since adult dogs will eat twice a day.

DOGS WEIGHT	AMOUNT PER DAY
3 pounds	1/3 cup to 1/2 cup
5 pounds	1/2 cup to 2/3 cup
10 pounds	3/4 cup to 1 cup
20 pounds	1 1/4 cups to 1 3/4 cups

Commercial dog food vs. homemade

It's been several years since the major recall of dog food that was laced with melamine. Melamine is an industrial chemical that can cause kidney stones, kidney failure, and finally death in animals and humans. The FDA does not approve melamine to be used in any food products for human or animal consumption. This giant recall moved many pet owners to begin to make their own dog food.

Let us see how commercial dog food compares to homemade dog food.

The FDA Center for Veterinary Medicine requires that pet food be "pure and wholesome" and "safe to eat for animals," but the pet food does not need approval from the FDA before being placed on the shelves to purchase. This allows the commercial pet food companies a huge amount of leeway in what is put into their pet food.

"By-products" is a common expression used on the list of ingredients on the dog food bag, which could be ground up sick animals, blood, chicken beaks and feet. Also, the ingredient list might say it contains vegetables, but most use fillers such as corn or beet pulp that are not healthy for your dog.

The FDA allows certain additives and preservatives for pet food that are considered to be unsafe for human consumption. These additives and preservatives are known to cause serious health problems such as cancer, kidney failure, liver failure and much more.

Homemade dog food actually is "wholesome and pure" and "safe to eat for animals" because we know what is in it. We don't give our pets ground up sick animals or fillers that are full of sugar. We choose high quality ingredients that we would eat ourselves.

Also, home-cooked dog food will be made fresh, and then frozen for our pet to enjoy in the next week or two. It will not be sitting on the grocery store shelves for the next year or two. Thus, it has no need for unnatural additives and preservatives.

Many commercial dog foods contain fillers. What are fillers? Fillers are ingredients such as corn or soy that have no nutritional value for your Maltipoo and are not absorbed by your dog's body because they have been processed so much that they are not really food.

Why do commercial dog food manufacturers use fillers? They use them to bulk up the food so it looks like you are getting more for your money. Also, it makes your dog full, but full of fake food that doesn't have any real nutrients, vitamins or minerals.

If you decide to purchase a commercial dog food, ask yourself while reading the ingredient list if you would eat that. If you would, then it is safe to feed your Maltipoo. You want to give your dog the best and that isn't usually what's on sale at the supermarket. You may have to look at your local pet supply store or order online.

Advantages of choosing a wholesome commercial brand dog food:

Shop around at your local pet supply store or online. There are some terrific commercial brand dog foods that use fresh whole foods and avoid the use of chemicals, preservatives and artificial flavors.

- **Convenience**: There is no preparation or cleanup needed. You just need to put it in your Maltipoo's dish, and voila!, dinner is served.
- **Training**: With obedience training, quite a bit of food is used and it is easier to use a pre-bought treat or dry kibble than to give it a handful of stew or mush. You can keep these treats out at room temperature and in your pocket, so you can easily reward it every time it responds correctly.
- **Peace of mind**: Home-cooked food can add extra stress and anxiety as the pet owner might wonder if the dog is receiving the correct balance of nutrients needed to grow and develop and having its daily nutritional needs met.
- **Cost-effectiveness**: Time is money. Not all of us have extra time to make our dog homemade dog food. Also, the homemade dog food will only be as healthy and wholesome as the ingredients we use, and using high-quality meats and organic free-range chicken quickly adds up in price.

Disadvantages of choosing a commercial brand dog food:

This list refers to the generic brands that are so common at the supermarket and have a long list of ingredients that you can't even pronounce.

- **Bloat**: Many generic dog food brands contain fillers that can cause your Maltipoo to become bloated. If you find your dog suffers from bloat, it might do better with a wet or canned food.
- **Boredom**: Even though your dog only has around 1700 taste buds and we humans have more than 9000, it can be boring to eat the same thing every single day.
- **Questionable ingredients**: Many of the ingredients are fillers, sugar, and ground up animals that might have been sick with tumors and other diseases. And artificial flavors, chemicals and preservatives can cause your Maltipoo to have serious physical and behavioral issues.
- **Obesity**: Many dogs suffer from obesity, which leads to other health problems. It is hard to control your Maltipoo's weight with a generic commercial dog food, as many of the ingredients are jam-packed with sugar and trans-fats.

Advantages of homemade dog food:

- **Peace of mind**: You know exactly what you are feeding your Maltipoo, since you are the chef. It is made fresh, so the ingredients haven't lost their nutritional value. By controlling the ingredients, you control your Maltipoo's exposure to chemicals and other harmful additives.

- **Limited ingredients**: If your Maltipoo suffers from food allergies, you can control its exposure to problem foods.
- **Cost-effectiveness**: Many pet owners who decide to make their own dog food use ingredients that they purchase for their family. Also, they make their dog's meals at the same time that they make their family's meals.

Disadvantages of homemade food:

- Daily nutrition concerns: Many pet owners that make their own dog food worry about whether their dog is receiving the correct amount of daily nutrients in its diet. Some studies have shown that dogs fed a homemade dog food diet suffer from nutritional deficiencies.
- Shelf life: Because all the ingredients are fresh, they tend to spoil fast and encourage bacterial growth and food borne illness.
- Cost: Depending on the ingredients you use, it can become quite costly to make your Maltipoo's food.

The choice ultimately is yours if you decide to buy your dog food or make your own dog food.

Never let someone else pressure you into doing something that you are not 100 percent convinced about. Your Maltipoo is your responsibility and nobody else's; you need to give it a diet that works for both of you.

How to choose a wholesome commercial dog food

Have you ever taken the time to look at the ingredient list for the dog food you feed your Maltipoo? Most of us trust the name on the packaging, believing it to be full of wholesome ingredients.

Others might have grown up seeing their parents feed the same brand to their dogs and they were never sick. But times have changed and many commercial dog food companies try to increase their profit margin by cutting corners, using fillers and preservatives.

Take the time to read the ingredient label before you feed your Maltipoo a certain brand of dog food. If you see one of these eight ingredients on the ingredient list, it is a red flag to put the bag back on the shelf and continue looking.

1. **BHA or BHT**: BHA is short for butyrate hydroxyanisole and BHT is short for butyrate hydroxytoluene. Why should they be avoided? They are both harmful preservatives used to extend the shelf life of

commercial dog food. These two ingredients are considered to be harmful because they have been directly linked to kidney and heart damage and cancer.

2. **Meat by-products**: What do meat by-products contain? The FDA's only labeling requirement for animal feed that contains meat by-products is that the by-products be from any animal source. What does this mean? It can be a mixture of anything from animal eyes, hooves, feet, beaks, feathers, blood, sick animals and any other kind of animal waste. Many times the sick animals that are ground up into the mixture have tumors or other illnesses.

Exception: Only buy the food if the packaging specifies that the by-products have been made from human-grade organ meats, such as livers and kidneys.

3. **Ethoxyquin**: Ethoxyquin is a pesticide and food preservative that has been banned for human consumption, as it has been directly linked to causing cancer. It is, however, commonly used as a preservative in commercial dog foods that contain fishmeal. A scary fact about ethoxyquin is that manufacturers are not required to include it on the ingredient list.

Exception: When looking for a dog food that contains fish, look for a written guarantee that it doesn't contain ethoxyquin. It should be on the packaging or their website. If it doesn't have a written statement, it most likely contains ethoxyquin, so put it back on the shelf.

4. **Corn**: Yes, corn! Corn is used as a cheap filler that has almost no nutritional value and can easily develop fungus or mold, causing your little Maltipoo to become very sick.

5. **Propyl Gallate**: It is also called Gallic Acid and Propyl Ester; this ingredient has been linked to liver disease and cancer.

6. **Con syrup**: Corn syrup, as we know, is extremely harmful for our dogs and us. It is used to sweeten commercial dog food to mask the flavor of the chemicals and by-products. It is an unnecessary ingredient that has absolutely no nutritional value. It can also cause your dog to become addicted to sugar and sweets leading to unwanted weight gain, diabetes, tooth decay, behavioral problems and hyperactivity.

7. **Soy**: Soy is another cheap filler used to boost the protein content in low-quality dog food. Soy has been linked to damage of the canine endocrine system.

8. **Artificial colors and flavors**: We all know that artificial colors and flavors are bad for us, and they are even more so for our dogs. Any ingredient list that has the word "artificial" in it should be avoided.

Artificial colors and flavors have been linked to cancer and mental and behavioral issues.

It pays in the long run to invest in a higher quality dog food with ingredients that are wholesome and pure. Know what you are really feeding your dog. You will be saving money in the future by preventing your Maltipoo from developing serious health problems.

How to choose a high-quality commercial brand dog food:

When it comes to choosing a dog food, the options seem endless. Here are some tips to narrow down your choices.

1. Superior source of protein: The main ingredient on the label should be a single source of protein, such as chicken meal or beef meal.

Photo Courtesy of Valentina Hartman

Avoid poultry meal or meat meal, which are vague and probably a lower quality protein.

2. Whole-meat source as the first two or three ingredients: Example: Chicken, chicken meal or Beef, beef meal. A good mix of meat proteins helps round out your Maltipoo's amino acids.

3. Whole, unprocessed grains and vegetables: The more processed the food is, the less nutritional value it has.

4. Expiration date: Look at the date of production and the expiration date. If it has a shelf life of two or more years, just put it back on the shelf and move on to a different brand.

5. Ingredient list: The longer the list, the faster you need to get away from that brand of dog food.

6. Canned dog food: Canned dog food might be more expensive, but it is a great option. It has the highest nutritional value and contains high-quality cuts of meat. Often it contains very few preservatives or chemicals.

How to make a wholesome homemade dog food

Some Maltipoo owners opt to make their homemade food, but also supplement with a high-quality commercial brand dog food.

At the end of this chapter, you will find some scrumptious dog food recipes that are worth trying. The recipes using the crock-pot are big time savers.

What are the proportions of a good recipe for homemade dog food?
- **40 – 50 percent protein**: Poultry, beef, lamb, fish or pork. You can add up to 10 percent of this by using organs such as liver or hearts. Make sure the meat you use is high-quality and fresh.

- **25 – 30 percent vegetables**: Make sure they are well cooked and finely chopped; dogs have a hard time digesting raw vegetables. You can use green beans, carrots, peas, broccoli, spinach and sweet potatoes.

- **25 –30 percent starch**: Brown or white rice, oats or pasta. If your Maltipoo is gluten intolerant, you can use gluten-free pasta.

Before using a new recipe, make sure none of the ingredients on the list are toxic for your little Maltipoo. Also, make sure that the proportions are in agreement with the above recommendations.

Tips for making homemade dog food

Here are some helpful tips for making homemade dog food:

1. After reading the information above about the threats found in commercial dog food, most of us will want to begin to feed our dog homemade meals immediately. But hold your horses! Changing your dog's food too fast can cause it to have diarrhea or an upset tummy. Switch your Maltipoo's dog food slowly!

   Gradually change the diet by mixing the new homemade food with the old commercial dog food. Slowly phase out the processed food.

2. Take time to prepare your dog food. Find a time to make the meals and give yourself time to put everything in freezer bags, measured in appropriate portions for your dog. Just as when cooking for your family, use safe food handling practices, especially if using raw meats.

3. Buy ingredients in bulk to save money, so your homemade dog food won't end up being much more expensive than commercial dog food.

4. Buy organic and high-quality ingredients. The food will only be as wholesome as the ingredients you use. Choose good high-quality meats and organic chicken, whenever possible.

5. You can prepare the homemade dog food in larger batches and just freeze them in daily portion sizes, saving time and energy.

6. Many Maltipoo owners who have chosen to make home cooked meals for their dogs also give them a multivitamin. Ask your veterinarian to recommend a multivitamin or supplement for your Maltipoo.

7. An important point to remember is portion control. Even though homemade food is wholesome and healthy, too much of a good thing can cause weight gain, which will lead to future health problems.

In order to choose the right home cooked diet for your Maltipoo, observe its reaction. Is it happy when it sees the meal? Does it happily gulp the food down? It doesn't matter how nutritious a meal is, if it goes uneaten it serves no nutritional value for your Maltipoo. Make food that is healthy but delicious for your little bundle of fur.

Here is a list of foods commonly used in homemade dog food:
- Whole eggs
- Carrots, cooked until tender
- Chicken, turkey, beef and pork without the fat
- Oats
- Sweet potatoes
- Peanut butter

- Plain yogurt
- Cottage cheese
- Pumpkin
- Apples, without the seeds
- Green beans
- Salmon

Why consider making your Maltipoo's meals?

There are many reasons to make your own home-cooked dog food. It is a healthier way to feed your dog, and can even be cheaper. In the past few years many dangerous additives and by-products that are being added to our pets' food have been brought to light.

Also, many dogs are developing illnesses that come with a high veterinary bill, such as: gluten intolerance, leaky gut, allergies, irritable bowel syndrome and other issues. These health issues have been directly linked to diet and most dog owners notice a quick improvement once they begin making their own healthy, balanced dog food. In a short time, these issues usually completely disappear and the vet bills are reduced too.

Feeding your dog is no more difficult than feeding your child. You just need to know some guidelines of how to feed it and what not to feed it.

One main reason many dog owners decide to make home-cooked meals is because they love their pets. We want our family members to have long, healthy lives. The same applies for our four-legged adopted members of the family.

Ask yourself:

- Would you consider serving your family, especially the little ones, only canned and processed foods?
- Would you feed them the same thing every day?

Most of us wouldn't even consider doing that, because we know it isn't healthy. Considering this point, why would we feed our dogs only canned and processed dry dog food?

It is important for all living creatures to eat fresh, whole foods appropriate for their species. Logically, to feed any living creature processed and canned foods for its entire life would not be a good choice.

These commercial, processed dog foods were created for our convenience and have been made popular thanks to mass advertising.

We could compare these processed dog food companies to the many fast-food establishments that surround us in our neighborhoods.

Yes, they are convenient, but are they healthy? How would our health be if we ate there every single day?

The answer is simple; we would be in dire need of a doctor in no time.

Maybe your lifestyle doesn't allow making your Maltipoo homemade dog food but do try some of the fantastic biscuit recipes in this chapter for your Maltipoo. They will be a big hit.

Foods to avoid

What foods should my dog never eat?

There are certain foods you should never feed your dog, no matter how much you love them yourself. There are some foods their stomachs can't digest properly, causing them pain or discomfort; there are others that are actually poisonous for them.

Here is a list of foods that you should never feed your beloved pet:
- Chocolate: a little bit of chocolate can wreak havoc on your dog's system, causing it to vomit and have diarrhea. A large amount can lead to heart failure and finally death.
- Garlic, onions, leeks and chives can be very toxic for dogs. They can cause anemia, making your dog very weak and elevating the heart rate, causing it to collapse.
- Cinnamon can irritate the inside of your dog's mouth, causing sores. Also, it can lower blood sugar, leading to diarrhea, vomiting and liver disease. If inhaled in powder form it can cause respiratory distress.
- Raisins and grapes can lead to kidney failure because they contain a toxin that causes severe liver and kidney damage.
- Almonds, pecans, macadamia and walnuts are toxic for dogs. Macadamia nuts are the most poisonous food for dogs, affecting the nervous system. Almonds can tear the esophagus and windpipe.
- Salt increases water retention, which can lead to heart disease and failure.
- Alcohol can cause intoxication, lack of coordination, and poor breathing and can lead to a coma or death.
- Cooked bones of any kind can easily splinter when chewed by your dog causing damage to the esophagus and windpipe. Raw bones are good for your dog's health and teeth.
- Coffee has the same effect on your dog as chocolate does.
- Corn on the cob blocks your dog's intestines and will have to be removed surgically.
- Yeast, on its own or in dough, can cause flatulence and discomfort; too much will cause the stomach to rupture.

- Xylitol is a sugar substitute in many food items today; it has no effect on humans but it is toxic for your dog. The smallest amount can cause seizures and death.
- Sugar in small amounts is tolerable but too much sugar can lead to obesity, dental problems and diabetes.
- Plums, peaches, pears and persimmons can be a choking hazard. Also, pear seeds contain arsenic, and peach pits, when metabolized, turn into cyanide.
- Liver is fine in very small doses but in large quantities it can cause adverse affects on your dog's muscles and bones.
- Avocadoes contain a toxin that causes dogs to have diarrhea, vomiting and heart congestion.

An excellent suggestion would be to make sure the whole family understands what the dog cannot eat. This will prevent someone sneaking it a treat that could cause serious damage or death.

The short list of foods above is not meant to be comprehensive. If you are in doubt about a food item that is not on the list, please check with your veterinarian before giving it to your dog.

Dog food recipes for your Maltipoo

Here is a small selection of wholesome dog food recipes for your Maltipoo puppy.

SINFULLY DELICIOUS TURKEY OR CHICKEN DOG FOOD

Your Maltipoo pup won't know how to thank you for this delicious dog food. It will be devoured in seconds.

INGREDIENTS
- 1 1/2 cups of plain rice, uncooked
- 1 tablespoon olive oil
- 3 pounds of ground turkey or chicken
- 3 cups of spinach, rinsed and finely chopped
- 2 large carrots, shredded
- 1 medium sized zucchini, shredded, or 1 cup of shredded pumpkin
- 1/2 cup of peas, frozen
- 1/2 cup of chicken or turkey broth, unsalted

INSTRUCTIONS
1. Cook the rice in a large pot according to the instructions on the package. Set aside.

2. In a pot, cook the ground turkey or chicken in the oil until fully cooked while breaking up any lumps.

3. Add the rest of the ingredients and cook together over low heat until the broth has almost evaporated and the vegetables are fully cooked, about 10 minutes.

4. Add the rice and thoroughly mix together. Let cool completely.

DOGGY BEEF STEW

This will be one of your pup's favorite meals. It will be licking its lips even before it is served.

INGREDIENTS
- 1 pound of stewing beef, chopped to pea-sized
- 1 small sweet potato, precooked and chopped
- 1/2 cup of carrots, precooked and diced
- 1/2 cup of green beans, precooked and diced
- 1/2 cup of flour (or ¼ cup of corn starch, if your dog is gluten intolerant)
- 1/2 cup of olive oil

INSTRUCTIONS
1. In a large pot, cook the stewing beef in 1 tablespoon olive oil until browned and dry, about 10 to 15 minutes.

2. Remove the cooked meat from the pot, reserving the drippings. Add the flour and the rest of the olive oil to the drippings in the pot. Whisk together over low heat until a thick gravy is formed. (If using corn starch, it should first be mixed into a small amount of cool water.)

3. Add, the meat and the precooked vegetables. Stir until everything is evenly coated.

4. Serve when cool.

RAW DOG FOOD RECIPE

Raw dog food can be easily digested by your dog and is very nutritious for any type of dog.

INGREDIENTS
- 2 1/2 pounds of high-quality sirloin steak, finely chopped
- 4 ounces of chicken livers,
- 1 carrot, finely shredded
- 1 small apple, cored
- 1/2 cup of spinach, rinsed

- 2 whole eggs
- 1/2 cup of plain yogurt or cottage cheese
- 1 tablespoon flax seed
- 1 tablespoon olive oil

INSTRUCTIONS

1. Place the carrot, apple and spinach into a food processor, and process until everything is finely chopped.
2. Add all of the remaining ingredients, except the chopped steak. Process again until everything is finely chopped and evenly combined.
3. Add all of the ingredients to a large bowl with the chopped steak. Mix everything together, using your hands.
4. Form into patties for your pup, taking into consideration its size, age and breed. Place on parchment paper and freeze. Freeze patties until solid and then transfer to a sealable freezer bag.
5. The night before serving, take out of the freezer a day's worth of patties and thaw in your fridge.

DOGGY CHILI

Your Maltipoo pup will love this protein-packed meal that will help it stay healthy and fit.

INGREDIENTS

- 4 organic chicken breasts
- 1 cup of unsalted kidney beans, drained
- 1 cup of unsalted black beans, drained
- 1 cup of carrots, finely diced or shredded
- 1/2 cup of tomato paste
- 4 cups of chicken broth, unsalted

INSTRUCTIONS

1. Cut the chicken into pea-sized pieces.
2. Place the chicken in a skillet, and cook over medium heat with a small amount of olive oil.
3. Mix all the ingredients in a large pot. Bring to a boil and boil for 10 minutes or until the carrots are very tender.
4. Turn off the heat. Let cool and freeze in daily portions for your puppy.

CROCK POT CHICKEN DOG FOOD

This will be one of your favorite recipes because it is so quick and easy to make, plus your pooch will love it.

INGREDIENTS
- 2 1/2 pounds of boneless, skinless chicken thighs and breasts
- 1 large sweet potato, diced in small pieces about the size of a pea
- 2 cups of frozen peas
- 2 cups of frozen green beans
- 1 large apple, cored and diced in small pieces about the size of a pea
- 1 can of unsalted kidney beans, drained
- 2 tablespoons of olive oil

INSTRUCTIONS
1. Place the chicken in the slow cooker and add water until it is just covered. Then top with the sweet potato, carrots, kidney beans, green beans and apple.
2. Cook on low heat for 8-9 hours; when almost finished add the frozen peas. Cook for an additional 30 minutes.
3. Drain off the excess liquid; add the olive oil and mash together with a spoon, breaking up the chicken pieces.
4. Let cool. Scoop into daily serving portions and freeze in freezer bags. Thaw in the fridge overnight before serving.

SLOW COOKER PORK DOG FOOD

The minute you put this delicious meal in your puppy's dish, it will come running.

INGREDIENTS
- 3 pounds pork tenderloin
- 2 large yams, cut into large pieces
- 1 bag of peas, frozen
- 2 apples, peeled and cored
- 1 can of unsalted kidney beans, drained
- 3 heads of broccoli, broken into smaller pieces
- 2 cups of spinach, rinsed and finely chopped

INSTRUCTIONS
1. Place the meat in the slow cooker; add water until just covered.
2. Place on top the yams, apples, carrots, broccoli and beans. Cook on low heat for 7-8 hours or on high heat for 5-6 hours; add the frozen peas when almost done. Cook for 30 minutes more.

3. Add the finely chopped spinach right at the end and cook 10 more minutes or until the spinach is cooked. The pork should shred easily. Mash the ingredients together.

4. Let cool. Scoop individual portions into freezer bags and freeze. Thaw overnight in the fridge before serving.

DOGGY MEATLOAF

Who doesn't enjoy a good old-fashioned meatloaf? Your pup is no exception. This meatloaf recipe will make your puppy smile all day long.

INGREDIENTS
- 1 pound of lean ground beef
- 2 eggs
- 1 1/2 cups of rolled oats
- 1/2 cup of cottage cheese
- 1 1/2 cups of mixed frozen vegetables

INSTRUCTIONS
1. Preheat oven to 350F.
2. Mix all the ingredients together until evenly combined; it is easiest to mix together using your hands. Press into a greased loaf pan.
3. Bake for 40 minutes or until done.
4. Let cool. Cut into slices for easy serving. Freeze.

Biscuit recipes for your Maltipoo

We all love junk food and an occasional treat, but we realize the majority of the snacks on the market today are jam-packed with chemicals and trans fats and are extremely high in calories. Most of us take the time to carefully read the ingredient list before we decide to dig in, steering clear of ingredients that we are unable to pronounce.

Many parents opt to just make homemade snacks for their children as a way to ensure that their children eat healthy. What about the commercial brand treats you buy for your Maltipoo? Should you be cautious?

As we have already learned, many commercial brand dog foods use fillers, sugar and preservatives. Treats are no exception; actually, manufacturers tend to cut even more corners with the treats, because there are no dietary requirements. Many brands use fructose, glucose and other sweeteners that your pup doesn't need.

There are some great doggy biscuits and treats on the market. You just need to do your research before you purchase a product. But for those that have the time and desire to make your own doggy treats for your Maltipoo, here is a list of some fast and easy recipes that your dog will love.

BACON PEANUT BUTTER TREATS

Bacon and peanut butter are every dog's favorite treat. Your pup will be begging for more!

INGREDIENTS

- 1 cup of creamy peanut butter, unsalted and unsweetened
- 3/4 cup of milk
- 1 egg
- 2 cups of whole wheat flour or a gluten-free substitute
- 1 tablespoon baking powder
- 1/3 cup of whole oats
- 3 strips of bacon, cooked and chopped into small pieces

INSTRUCTIONS

1. Preheat the oven to 325*F. Lightly grease your cookie sheets.
2. In a bowl, combine the peanut butter, milk, oats and eggs until thoroughly combined.
3. Add the flour, baking powder and bacon pieces. Mix until just combined. It will be a stiff dough and you might have to knead the dough to combine all the ingredients.
4. On a lightly floured countertop, roll out the dough to about 1cm thick. Cut with a cookie cutter shaped like a bone (or any shape you like). Make sure the cookies are no bigger than 3cm. Arrange evenly on the cookie tray.
5. Bake for 18 to 20 minutes, then take the cookies out the oven and flip over each cookie on the tray. Place back in the oven for 10 minutes or until lightly browned. This will make a crunchy biscuit that will last a long time and be good for your Maltipoo's teeth.
6. Let cool before you give your pup a treat. Store at room temperature for a week or freeze up to 3 months.

D.I.Y MALTIPOO ICECREAM

I scream, you scream, we all scream for ice cream! Your Maltipoo pup will love these treats during the hot summer months.

INGREDIENTS

- 1 quart of plain yogurt
- 2 ripe bananas
- 1/2 cup of creamy peanut butter, unsweetened and unsalted

INSTRUCTIONS
1. Combine all the ingredients in a food processor. Pulse until smooth.
2. Place into small containers (such as an ice cube tray) and freeze.
3. Pop out of the containers and store in a bag in the freezer.

JERKY CHICKEN OR BEEF CHEWS

This will be one of your pup's favorite snacks, especially when it is teething.

INGREDIENTS
- 2 pounds of chicken breasts or good-quality steak
- Oil, as needed

INSTRUCTIONS
1. Preheat oven to 200F.
2. Cut the chicken or steak into long thin strips, the thinner the better.
3. Lightly grease a rack with a cookie sheet underneath to catch the drippings. Evenly space the chicken or beef strips on the rack, allowing space around each one so they can dry out properly.
4. Cook in the oven for about 2 hours, then flip them over and cook for about 30 minutes to an hour more or until totally dried out. Some of the thicker pieces will take longer.
5. Store in the fridge or freeze.

NO BAKE PUPPY SNACKS

This is a perfect recipe for those hot summer days when you don't feel like turning on the oven.

INGREDIENTS
- 3/4 cup creamy peanut butter, unsalted and unsweetened
- 2 ripe bananas, mashed
- 1 1/4 cups of rolled oats

INSTRUCTIONS
1. Cover a cookie sheet with plastic wrap and set aside.
2. In a bowl, mix all of the ingredients until thoroughly combined.
3. Form the mixture into balls about 2 cm in diameter. Place on the cookie sheet.
4. Chill the balls in the fridge for 1-3 hours or until firm. Store in a ziplock bag in the freezer.

BANANA CARROT TREATS

These biscuits are jam-packed with wholesome goodness for your Maltipoo.

INGREDIENTS
- 1 cup whole wheat flour (or a gluten-free substitute of your choice)
- 1 cup oats
- 1 ripe banana, mashed
- 2 carrots, finely shredded
- 2 tablespoons olive oil
- 1 tablespoon brown sugar
- 1 tablespoon parsley, chopped
- 1 egg

INSTRUCTIONS
1. Preheat oven to 350*F.
2. Place all of the ingredients in a bowl and mix until thoroughly combined.
3. On a lightly floured surface, roll out the dough to about 1/2 inch thick.
4. Cut with cookie cutters.
5. Place on a lightly greased cookie sheet.
6. Bake for 30 minutes or less, depending on the size.
7. For a softer cookie, take out of the oven after baking. For a crunchy cookie, turn off the oven after baking and leave in the oven for 30 minutes more. This will dry out the cookies, making a crunchy snack for your puppy.
8. Let cool. Store at room temperature for one week or in the freezer for 3 months.

PEANUT BUTTER SANDWICH COOKIES

These snacks will get your puppy in the festive mood for the holidays. They are a little more time-consuming to make, so they can be for a special occasion.

INGREDIENTS
- 1 1/4 cups of flour (or a gluten-free substitute of your choice)
- 1/2 teaspoon of baking powder
- 1/2 cup of creamy peanut butter, unsalted and unsweetened
- 1 egg
- 2 tablespoons of honey
- 1/2 cup of milk

- Additional creamy peanut butter, to sandwich the cookies together

INSTRUCTIONS
1. Preheat the oven to 350*F.
2. Place all of the ingredients in a bowl (except the extra peanut butter for sandwiching the cookies together)
3. Mix everything together until thoroughly combined.
4. On a lightly floured surface, roll out the dough to about 1 inch thick. Cut into the desired shapes and sizes. Place on a lightly oiled cookie sheet.
5. Bake for about 10-12 minutes or until they have a uniform color. Cool.
6. Place in a freezer bag and freeze. Whenever you want to give your Maltipoo a festive treat, just smear some peanut butter on the bottom side of one of the cookies and sandwich together with another cookie.
7. It is recommended to sandwich the cookies together just before serving to prevent the cookies from getting soggy.

APPLE, CHEDDAR AND BACON BISCUITS

Your Maltipoo will be on its best behavior in hopes of getting one of these scrumptious biscuits. Get ready for some serious tail wagging!

INGREDIENTS
- 1 2/3 cups of flour
- 1 1/2 cups of whole wheat flour
- 1 egg
- 1/4 cup of softened butter or olive oil, or a combination of both
- 1 large apple, cored, peeled and grated
- 2 tablespoons of parsley, chopped
- 3 pieces of bacon, cooked and crumbled
- 1 cup of cheddar cheese, grated
- 1 cup of milk

INSTRUCTIONS
1. Preheat oven to 350*F.
2. In a bowl, place all of the ingredients and mix until thoroughly combined.
3. On a lightly floured surface, roll out the dough to about 1/4 inch thick.
4. If desired, as you roll out the dough, sprinkle extra cheese and bacon bits on top to make the treats look even more delicious.
5. Cut into the desired shapes. Place evenly on a lightly oiled cookie sheet.
6. Bake for 20 to 30 minutes, depending on the size.
7. Cool completely. Store at room temperature for one week or in the freezer for 3 months.

CHAPTER EIGHT
Maltipoos and their Health

Since Maltipoos are a newer breed, there isn't a long list of maladies that are commonly associated with them. But there are some common concerns that seem to pop up every once in a while with Maltipoos, mostly related to their Poodle and Maltese ancestry. We will discuss some of these issues in this chapter.

Being aware of these issues can help you prevent them, and if they do occur, you will be able to recognize the symptoms in time and take your Maltipoo to the veterinarian for a check-up.

When in doubt, call your veterinarian about any questions or concerns you may have about your Maltipoo's health. It is better to be safe than sorry. Because of their size, Maltipoos are very delicate, and when they get sick, it can progress very fast.

When to call your veterinarian:
- Change in temperament: Watch for changes in appetite or energy levels (lethargy).
- Limping: It might favor one paw over another, have a limp, or refuse to stand up, even when bribed with a treat.
- Difficulty breathing: If your Maltipoo looks like it is gagging or cannot breathe, check its airways and call your veterinarian.
- Excessive drooling: Some dogs drool while watching people eat; excessive drooling is when your dog drools for no apparent reason and doesn't stop.
- Neurological conditions: Your Maltipoo is normally alert and responsive. A sign of neurological problems is when your dog becomes disoriented, unresponsive, severely uncoordinated, lethargic or even goes into a coma.
- Seizures: If your Maltipoo has never experienced a seizure before, it needs to see a veterinarian as soon as possible. Seizures can manifest as uncontrollable shaking, tremors, loss of consciousness, and possible loss of bowel control.
- Toxic exposure: If you know your dog was exposed to a something toxic or a food item that is toxic for dogs, immediately take your dog to the veterinarian.
- Vomiting and diarrhea: If the vomiting and diarrhea continue longer than 24 hours call your veterinarian.

- Distended abdomen or abdominal pain: If you notice your dog having dry heaves, retching, weakness, collapsing and troubles breathing is likely your dog is suffering from bloat. It is more common in large dogs, but does occur occasionally with smaller dogs. This is a life-threatening problem if not quickly treated by your veterinarian.
- Urinary problems: If you notice that your dog tries to go pee but is unable to, it might have a urinary blockage.

This is just a basic list of some of the health issues that might warrant an emergency visit to the veterinarian's office. If there is something wrong with your dog, remember your veterinarian is only a phone call away. Don't be afraid to pick up the phone and ask if there is a reason to be concerned.

Photo Courtesy of
Lisa Lynch

Vaccinations

" *It is very important to have your puppy checked by your vet within a few days of bringing it home. He should verify that the puppy is healthy and let you know what vaccinations will be required, before you can expose your puppy to other dogs."*

Rebecca Posten
riversidepuppies.biz

Your veterinarian can explain the vaccination schedule for your Maltipoo. Normally, they will give you a small handbook, which has the age of your dog, a schedule for when it should receive each vaccination, and the length of immunity.

Vaccinations are divided into two different categories. The main ones are called "core vaccines" and these are vaccines that every dog should receive. The second category is called "non-core vaccines"-- these are only recommended for certain dogs in certain parts of the United States.

Below is a typical vaccination schedule for dogs; ask for a copy of the schedule used by your veterinarian. Most veterinarians send out reminders to their clients before it is time for the vaccines.

DOG VACCINE SCHEDULE	
Age	**Vaccination**
5 weeks	**Parvovirus**: Puppies are at high risk for this virus.
6 and 8 weeks	Combined vaccine: often called a 5-way vaccine for adenovirus cough, hepatitis, distemper, parainfluenza and parvovirus; it might contain leptospirosis and coronavirus.
12 weeks	**Rabies**: Varies according to law in different states.
12 and 15 weeks	**Combined vaccine**: Containing leptospirosis, coronavirus and Lyme disease.
Adult (boosters)	**Combined vaccine**: Containing leptospirosis, coronavirus, Lyme and rabies

If you plan on using a kennel or sending your Maltipoo to doggy day care, it might be wise to get the vaccine for kennel cough. Kennel cough is a horrible dry cough that is very contagious and it commonly spreads in areas where there are lots of dogs, such as a kennel or doggy day care. Your dog can even catch it at the groomer.

For a more detailed explanation about the different vaccinations your Maltipoo will need, please talk to your veterinarian.

Neutering and spaying

Most likely, you are purchasing your Maltipoo as a companion pet and not to breed. Second generation Maltipoos don't have the same qualities as first generation Maltipoos, and since the Maltipoo is not a registered breed, there isn't a lot of profit in breeding them. Therefore, most Maltipoo owners decide to have their dogs spayed or neutered.

Spaying and neutering are simple procedures performed by your veterinarian, taking away your dog's ability to reproduce. They are very fast, simple and common operations for dogs.

Advantages to neutering your male Maltipoo:
- Less aggressive
- Less inclined to mark his territory
- Less competitive
- More likely to form a tight bond with his human owner
- Less territorial

Advantages to spaying your female Maltipoo:
- Doesn't go into heat
- Less nervous
- Barks and cries less
- No unwanted pregnancies

Advantages for both:
- Less inclined to roam
- Less aggressive
- Calmer and less hyperactive
- Less likely to escape
- More obedient

Studies have proven that dogs that have had these procedures are at a lower risk of cancer than dogs that did not receive these procedures.

What is neutering? Neutering is a procedure performed by a licensed veterinary surgeon. The operation will render your male dog unable to reproduce.

It is commonly referred to as castration because it removes the young dog's testicles, leaving behind an empty scrotal sac, which used to contain your dog's testicles. Over time, this sac will shrink in size until it is no longer noticeable.

When should my male Maltipoo be neutered? It is recommended to neuter dogs before six months of age to avoid unwanted weight gain when they are older. Maltipoos neutered after six months have the tendency to become quite obese.

He will also be less likely to wander if the operation is before he is six months old. Waiting longer than six months means your Maltipoo might have testosterone already built up inside of him. This testosterone will drive him to try to escape in search of a female to mate with.

Non-neutered males have the tendency to spray their pee around their living quarters, which includes your house. They do this to mark their territory; a neutered dog will not do this.

What is spaying? It is sterilization for female puppies, involving a simple procedure preformed by a licensed veterinarian surgeon. This procedure will prevent your dog from becoming pregnant and stop her regular heat cycles.

This surgery is a little more complicated than neutering male dogs. It involves removing both ovaries and the uterus by making a small incision into your puppy's abdomen. The uterus is removed to prevent future infections.

Photo Courtesy of
Joanna Howard

When should your female Maltipoo be spayed? Veterinarians suggest the best time is between four and six months of age, but it can be done later with no side effects.

Both spaying and neutering require a general anesthesia.

Spaying and neutering will not affect your dog's personality. Your dog will not resent you for this operation--he or she will just carry on with life as before the operation. These procedures can mellow out unfavorable personality traits, such as being aggressive.

Choosing to neuter or spay your Maltipoo is a personal decision. Talk to your veterinarian if you have any doubts or concerns.

Future health concerns and how to avoid them

66 *Making sure that your Maltipoo has plenty of exercise, maintains a healthy weight and has good oral hygiene will extend its lifespan."*

Rebecca Posten
riversidepuppies.biz

What follows is just a list of common illnesses that affect Maltipoos; it doesn't mean your Maltipoo will get them. It is just to help you be aware of them and of how you might be able to prevent your Maltipoo from suffering from them.

White Shaker Syndrome: This syndrome affects both Maltese and Poodles, so for obvious reasons your Maltipoo can have the same issue. It normally manifests itself when your puppy is about six months old.

Symptoms: Your dog will have tremors all over its body, lack of coordination and rapid eye movement.

It doesn't cause your dog any pain and will not change your dog's personality. It will, however, give you a panic attack the first time it happens. It normally happens when a dog gets overly excited or stressed. Talk to your veterinarian about how to treat it. If you are unsure whether your dog has White Shaker Syndrome, try to catch one of the episodes on camera and show it to your veterinarian.

Epilepsy: This is when your Maltipoo has a seizure.

Symptoms: Your dog will begin to shake uncontrollably for a few seconds or longer. It is suspected to be hereditary but that hasn't been scientifically proven yet.

Epilepsy cannot be cured but it can be treated effectively with medicine. A Maltipoo with epilepsy can live a long and happy life with no complications, if it is managed properly.

Patellar Luxation: Also called "slipped stifles." It is a common problem for all small dogs. It is caused when the patella, which is made up of three parts--the thighbone, kneecap and calf--are not properly lined up. This makes the leg become limp. It is considered to be a birth defect but doesn't present itself until later on in life. The rubbing of the unaligned bones can lead to arthritis or degenerative joint disease.

Symptoms: Walking with a limp or a skip or hop. In severe cases, surgical repair might be required.

It is more common with smaller dogs and can be a result of bad breeding practices.

Porto-systemic shunt: Occurs when there is an abnormal flow of blood between the liver and the body. This becomes a problem because the liver is responsible for detoxifying the body, metabolizing the nutrients found in the food, and other things. Signs of this disease appear around two years of age.

Symptoms: Symptoms could be neurobehavioral abnormalities (such as lack of balance), lack of appetite, hypoglycemia, stomach issues and stunted growth.

Your veterinarian might recommend corrective surgery or a special diet.

Progressive Retinal Atrophy: This is a hereditary degenerative eye disorder that will eventually cause blindness. It takes years before your dog begins to go blind.

Have your veterinarian do a simple test to tell if your dog has this disease.

The good news is that dogs can use their other senses when they go blind and still live a happy and full life.

Good breeders will have their breeding dogs certified yearly and do not breed dogs that carry this disease.

Legg-Calve-Perthes Disease: This is a common problem for toy dogs. The blood supply to the hipbone is decreased and the head of the hipbone that connects to the pelvis begins to disintegrate.

Symptoms: Normally manifests itself when a puppy is around four to six months old; it begins to limp and the leg muscles becomes stiff.

This condition can be corrected with surgery and the prognosis after surgery is very positive. Most dogs have almost no lameness, and if so, only when the weather changes.

Most of these health issues are hereditary, so before purchasing your Maltipoo, investigate whether the parents suffer from any of these issues. Both parents should have a clean bill of health certificate from the Orthopedic Foundation for Animals for patella (knees) and a certificate from the Canine Eye Registry Foundation certifying that their eyes are healthy.

Also, look for a breeder that doesn't begin to breed dogs until they are two or three years old, since many of these diseases manifest after two years of age.

How to choose a good veterinarian

The day you bring your little Maltipoo home is the day you promise that you are going to love and care for it for the rest of its life. It is a big responsibility, when you think about it.

Your puppy will depend on your for all of its basic needs, including medical care. How can you choose a good veterinarian?

Before you choose a veterinarian, sit down and ask yourself what qualities you would want in your Maltipoo's future medical doctor. Also make a list of questions that you would like to ask regarding your Maltipoo.

You can also ask the local shelter, breeders, and other dog owners for references for the veterinarian you are considering.

Make sure your veterinarian is approved by the American Animal Hospital Association. Many animal clinics are not approved by A.A.H.A., but this membership ensures a certain level of medical care for your Maltipoo.

When you meet the veterinarian do you pick up a positive vibe? Does he or she seem to love animals or just tolerate them?

A good veterinarian should have some basic equipment, such as an x-ray, ultrasound, IV pumps, and blood and eye pressure measuring tools, and also be able to do basic lab tests. Find out if there are any specialists working in the clinic.

Do the staff members working there seem knowledgeable and friendly? Do they like animals or just tolerate them? You will bring your baby here and you will be paying for a service; you should get what you pay for.

Make sure the veterinarian is available at all hours, in case of an emergency.

CHAPTER NINE
Common behavior issues

Dogs are not born bad. Like humans, they are influenced by their surroundings and their interactions with others. These surroundings and interactions can mold them in positive and negative ways.

Bad upbringing and bad training cause almost all dog behavior problems.

How to stop your Maltipoo from having bad habits

" *Maltipoos can be easily spoiled because of their adorable faces and small size. Barking can become an issue if you do not control it from the start."*

Renee Banovich
www.aTender1sPuppies.com

You need to clearly communicate to your dog what is expected of it in a way that it can understand. Plus that message needs to be consistent. You can't say "no" one day, then the next day say "yes." No means no and yes means yes. Your Maltipoo is very intelligent but it is unable to read between the lines. By not being consistent with training your dog, you will be only confusing it.

Also, without realizing it, you might be reinforcing bad behaviors. You need to learn to reward your dog for positive behavior and not bad behavior. Behavior that is not rewarded will slowly decrease and behavior that is rewarded will increase. So make sure you are rewarding the correct behavior.

Remember a large majority of dogs end up in shelters or abandoned between one to two years of age because of these bad habits. This is when the cuteness wears off and the behavior becomes very frustrating to the owner.

By applying these simple steps now, you will prevent bad behavior and heartache later on. It will lead to a long and happy life with your newfound best friend, your Maltipoo.

Jumping

Have you ever walked into a house and been greeted by an overly friendly dog that won't stop jumping on you? It is quite annoying, especially if you are wearing nylons or dress pants.

You really don't want your Maltipoo to jump on everyone that comes through the front door. The key is to stop your dog from jumping in the first place. If it already jumps, you will need to stop it from becoming a habit. The good news is that this bad habit is a very easy one to correct.

How to stop your Maltipoo from jumping:

Photo Courtesy of Amy Isett

1. Ignore your dog while it is jumping, even if it is hard to do. Only praise and reward it when it is not jumping.

2. Never, ever pet your Maltipoo when it is jumping. Petting is a type of praise and affection, which sends a message to its brain telling it that jumping is good behavior. This will reinforce jumping.

3. Once you see that it has all four paws on the floor, give it a treat for not jumping.

4. If you have taught your dog to lie down, give that command and then give it a treat and generously praise it.

5. Repeat the first three steps until you can walk into a room or the house without your Maltipoo jumping on you or other people.

Some Maltipoo owners have taught their dogs to dance; then when they begin to jump, they say the command "dance" and their Maltipoo does a little dance around the room instead of jumping on their legs.

Biting

Every year in the United States, dogs bite more than 4.5 million people. The ones bitten most often are children; second, the elderly; and third, the postman. Approximately twenty people die each year of complications from dog bites. Many dogs that bite someone have to be euthanized.

Biting should be discouraged from the very first day you bring your Maltipoo home. Puppies begin biting to relieve their teething discomfort and their sore gums.

Biting and chewing is considered common behavior for puppies but unacceptable for adult dogs. The key is teaching your puppy to be gentle.

Let's think about how puppies interact with each other. Puppies are just learning how to control their bodies and their strength. Many times, while playing with their littermates, they might bite too hard. What does the other puppy do? It yelps out in pain and the fun time comes to a halt. If the puppy bites its mom too hard, it might get a harsher lesson. That puppy will never ever bite its mom again.

❝ *Generally, they have a friendly disposition towards other dogs. They are territorial and will protect their homes, if other dogs try to enter it. In public places, such as parks, they are mostly friendly towards other dogs."*

Spencer Carranza
maltipoored.com

You need to teach your Maltipoo that it is inappropriate to bite humans. Never allow it to bite you or anyone else. Always stop it in the act, say a firm "No," and stop playing until it stops biting.

How can your discourage your Maltipoo from biting?

- Avoid playing aggressive games such as tug-o-war; instead play positive games like fetch and train your dog to drop the ball in front of you.
- When it begins to bite you or something that you don't want it to bite, firmly say "No" and remove the item or your hand and replace it with an acceptable chew toy.
- If it is overly persistent with biting and chewing, many trainers suggest the following technique to stop the biting. Put your thumb over your Maltipoo's tongue and gently hold the bottom part of its mouth with your four fingers. As you do this say "No" firmly, then release its mouth. Do not give it another chew toy. Repeat this process as necessary.
- If your puppy is determined to bite at all costs, begin hand feeding it. This will get it used to your hands being near its mouth and it will associate human skin with mealtime and not bite time. If it bites you, say "No" and close up your hand, then resume feeding once it has calmed down.
- Some dogs are so hyperactive they don't even realize they are biting. If this is the case, put Cheese Whiz or peanut butter on your hands

and your dog will begin to lick it off. Tell it as it approaches to lick it off, "Kisses." It will begin associate the word "kisses" with licking your hands instead of biting.

- If it bites particularly hard, yelp sharply like another puppy would, let your hand go limp, and stop playing. This will startle your puppy and it will stop biting you. If it continues biting you after two or three yelps, it is time to give your puppy a time out.

These suggestions to teach your Maltipoo to stop biting or chewing use positive reinforcement, never using force or yelling at your dog.

If your dog does bite you, resist the tendency to pull away from the bite. This will make your puppy believe you are playing tug-o-war and it will bite down even harder.

Never, ever smack or hit your dog on the nose for biting or chewing. This is a negative reinforcement that encourages it to bite even harder and is not an effective tool in obedience training.

Ankle biters

Most small dogs have the reputation of being ankle biters and Maltipoos are no exception. They are fascinated with biting at people's ankles as they walk. How can you stop your Maltipoo from learning this bad habit?

- Have one of your dog's favorite toys in your pocket and when it begins to nip at your heels or ankles, stop walking and give it the toy to play with.

- If you don't have a toy in your pocket and your Maltipoo begins to bite you while you are walking, stop walking. When it stops biting, offer it a treat or praise. The idea is for it to associate good things happening to it with good behavior.

The key is to nip nipping in the bud before it even becomes a problem.

Chewing

Chewing is one of the most common bad habits for Maltipoos. The key to avoid this bad habit is to begin teaching your Maltipoo not to chew on certain items from day one.

Puppies use their teeth to explore their new surroundings. This is normal behavior but it quickly becomes unwanted behavior when they chew on your shoes or furniture. If unwanted chewing isn't corrected when your Maltipoo is still a puppy, it can lead to costly destruction of your personal property, medical problems and trust issues between you and your dog.

Your Maltipoo will go on a chewing frenzy when it is teething. From four weeks to six months of age, your puppy will be going through a painful teething period. All puppies tend to chew more during this time period because their gums are irritated and chewing helps to relieve their discomfort. If this behavior isn't stopped during this time period, it will turn into a nightmare as your dog gets older. How can you prevent this from happening?

- Puppy-proof your home. Remove objects that might cause your puppy to become curious and begin chewing, such as shoes, socks or anything that seems chewable.

Photo Courtesy of
Mary Papadopoulos

- Encourage chewing on appropriate items. Each dog will have its own preferences as to the type of chew toys. You will need to experiment until you find its favorite.

- Don't give your Maltipoo an old shoe to chew on; it will not be able to tell the difference between a new or old shoe. Instead, it will think all shoes are fair game for chewing because you already gave it a shoe.

- If you find your Maltipoo chewing on an inappropriate object, correct it by taking the object away and saying a firm "No" as you remove it. Then give it an appropriate object to chew on. Praise it when it begins to chew on the right thing. Over time, your Maltipoo will learn what objects it can chew on and what objects it is not allowed to chew on.

- You can also apply deterrent sprays to objects that you don't want it chewing on, such as the furniture or kitchen table legs. This spray is non-toxic and leaves a disgusting taste in your dog's mouth, which will deter it from chewing on that object again. You can find this spray at your local pet supply store.

- A tired dog is less likely to chew. Dogs often begin to chew out of boredom. Make sure to play with your dog a lot.

Separation anxiety

Maltipoos thrive on human companionship. They quickly bond with their owners and depend upon them for everything. That is one of the characteristics that make Maltipoos the ideal companion dog. But this quality can sometimes work against you.

What is separation anxiety?

Separation anxiety is caused when your dog is left home alone and begins to feel anxiety from being separated from you. It is a serious matter that will have to be dealt with.

How does it manifest?

You dog might do one or all of the following to release its anxiety and stress:

1. **Destruction of your personal belongings**: It might go on a chewing frenzy, chewing on your couch pillows, the coffee table, your shoes; basically anything in its path will be chewed on, and if possible, devoured.

2. **Defecating and urinating inside your house**: This is one of the most unpleasant side effects of separation anxiety. It might go to the bathroom throughout your house because it is so upset and afraid of being abandoned by you.

3. **Barking and whining uncontrollably**: Your neighbors will hate you when this happens and secretly begin to look for a way to evict you and your dog from the building. No matter how exhausted your dog is, it will continue barking until someone comes to its rescue.

4. **Relentless scratching**: It might scratch at the doors, since that is where you disappeared and it believes that if it can just get outside it can find you.

5. **Pacing**: Some Maltipoos become so worked up that they begin intense, persistent pacing and become even more worked up.

6. **Physical issues**: With really severe separation anxiety, it might begin excessive panting which could lead to heart failure in extreme cases.

Separation anxiety can cause damage to your Maltipoo's mental and physical health. Behaviors that result from separation anxiety aren't happening because your dog is evil and is out to seek revenge for you leaving it alone. It is acting out because it is in a state of panic and fear from being separated from its pack leader, you.

In many cases owners encourage their Maltipoo to suffer from separation anxiety. How is this?

Making a big fuss every time you leave or come home essentially rewards your dog for missing you, as soon as you walk in the front door.

Photo Courtesy of
Veronica Gomes

This can reinforce its becoming anxious and stressed every time you leave or come home.

A puppy who is smothered with attention and taken everywhere you go learns to love being with you and never being left alone. Then, as it get older, the puppy charm begins to wear off and you suddenly stop spending so much time with it. It feels like it needs to be with you and doesn't understand why it is being left home alone. You have become its security blanket and pack leader.

Also, many times puppies are taught to act out when left alone, even if it is only for a few seconds. Here is an example of how that could happen:

From the very first day you bring your puppy home, it begins to experience separation anxiety because of being separated from its litter, its pack. You bring it home into strange new surroundings and you begin to become the new pack leader. You put it in the den or crate and walk away, and it begins to cry. What do you do? You go running and pick it up and tell it everything is okay. By doing that you are rewarding it for that behavior. You are teaching it that it is fine to cry.

From day one, you need to teach your Maltipoo to be quiet and learn to be alone for small periods of time. You can only reward good behavior such as being quiet and settled. When it is outside of its den, it isn't necessary to entertain it non-stop, but encourage it to play by itself. This will prepare it for when you leave it alone in the future.

Maltipoos dislike changes to their routines and that causes them have separation anxiety. That is when they become stressed and destructive.

To avoid your Maltipoo suffering from separation anxiety, you need to teach your puppy to trust you as the leader of the pack. It learns to trust you by being trusted by you, allowing it to have confidence in itself. Then when you leave it alone, it knows that you haven't abandoned it and you will be coming home.

Separation anxiety is a sign of how well you have trained your dog in all other aspects of obedience training. If you have trained your dog well and it is well-behaved, the chances of it suffering from separation anxiety are almost none.

How can you teach your Maltipoo to be left alone in the house without having a breakdown?
- Training takes time. Take time daily to show your Maltipoo what you expect of it and help it understand how it fits into your daily routine. Take every opportunity to train it. Two minutes here and there adds up to some high-quality training time.
- Teach your dog to lie on the floor, and then slip out of sight and come back. Each time you do this, increase the time between when

you slip away and when you come back. Don't make a big deal each time. Just act normal, and your dog will begin to realize that you haven't abandoned it and you always come back. This is a trust and confidence exercise.

- Both you and members of your family need to establish that you are the pack leaders and the dog isn't in control. For example, it will try to be in control by getting you to do things you weren't going to do, such as pet it. If it comes up to you and nudges your hand so that you pet it, it might seem so cute that you can't resist. But it was exerting itself and as the pack leader; it was in control. Then when it is in a situation such as being left at home alone, it realizes it isn't in control and stresses and begins to act out.
- Change can sometimes cause Maltipoos to experience separation anxiety. You can help your dog deal with change by shaking up your movements each day. We are all creatures of habit. If your Maltipoo tends to follow you around the house, when you get up to move to the other room and notice your pup stands up to follow you, just sit back down and it will too. Wait a bit and then go. Come in or out of the house through a different door. Put your shoes and bag in a different area. Your pup will notice these small changes and deal with them, which will help increase its confidence in itself to know that it will be fine alone.
- If you are crate training your Maltipoo, place the crate with your dog inside in the busiest part of the house and go about your activities. This will get it used to hearing everyday noises and movements without needing to be in the center of everything. It knows you are in charge as the pack leader and that you will protect it.
- Get your Maltipoo used to being left alone by lots of rehearsals. Walk out and return before it begins to cry or bark. Allow your dog to see you go through all of the movements that show you are leaving, such as putting on your shoes and your jacket; then leave briefly. When you come back in, calmly and indifferently greet your dog; then, give it a command such as "shake" or "sit" and give it a reward.

Suggestions to help your Maltipoo relax when left alone:
- Leave on the TV or music in the background for your Maltipoo while you go out and leave it alone. Most dogs like background noise and it can help them to feel more secure.
- If you leave your Maltipoo in a crate when you go out, try covering part of it with a blanket. This will feel more like a den and will make it feel secure and safe.
- Leave your dog playing with toys that are safe to use without supervision and will keep it distracted for some time. Toys that have treats

that are occasionally released are great because they keep your dog mentally stimulated and it will soon get tired and fall asleep.

- Before leaving your house, avoid giving it too much attention. All your Maltipoo understands is that all that love and attention were abruptly cut off, causing it to go into panic mode.

- Hide treats around the house; this will keep it occupied and prevent it from becoming bored while you are gone.

Separation anxiety is a sign that your Maltipoo loves and misses you. It doesn't want to see you to leave, but if you practice the above suggestions, it will not become stressed or frightened when you leave because it has learned to trust you and knows that you would never abandon it. That is true love; true love is based on trust and respect.

Socializing with other dogs

Some dogs, like some people, are extremely antisocial. Just greeting them can be an uncomfortable experience. Sometimes, this antisocial behavior was caused by not being exposed to people when they were children. Sometimes, it can be because of extreme shyness; but in either case, it is because they never learned to socialize with others.

Some dogs seem to get in fights with bigger dogs, no matter how tiny they are, because they have never properly learned how to socialize with other dogs. Dogs that haven't learned to socialize with other dogs will most likely grow up and be shy and skittish.

When is the best time to socialize your Maltipoo?

The best time to begin socializing your Maltipoo is while it is still a puppy. Puppies don't have any pre-established requirements or misconceptions about other dogs. They just see them as new playmates.

Choose your Maltipoo's new acquaintances carefully, making sure they have had their vaccinations, if your puppy hasn't yet. Make sure the dog you are going to introduce your puppy to is a friendly dog, so the experience will be positive.

How to socialize your dog with other dogs:

While you are out walking together is a wonderful time to introduce your Maltipoo pup to other dogs. Normally, when dogs are out for a walk, they have already released some of their pent-up energy, so they will be more calm and submissive.

If your Maltipoo begins to bark at another dog, don't pull back on the leash, as that will get it even more excited and worked up. It will remember this negative experience next time it meets a dog, and act the same.

If your dog begins to bark, do show a calm and assertive attitude and distract it to look somewhere else. If it doesn't stop barking, just pick it up, walk away, and try again later.

The dog park is a great way for your Maltipoo to meet new dogs, but it can be very intimidating at first. Expose it slowly to the Dog Park. The first week, you might walk around the park but not go in. If all the dogs are having fun inside the park, your Maltipoo will want to play with them. Each time you go back, go a little further inside, until you know your Maltipoo will not act like an antisocial grumpy dog.

Socializing with other humans

Have you ever gone over to your friend's house, and before you are even in the door, their hyper dog is jumping on you and barking? Other dogs lurk around like you are the devil and cannot be trusted under any circumstances. Some dogs go and hide from new people because they are extremely shy.

Surely you don't want your little Maltipoo to act like that, so how can you teach it to behave around strangers and your friends and family?

You want your Maltipoo not to be prejudiced against anyone. Some dogs are cautious about certain physical features, such as a beard, a cane, a hat or sunglasses. Others dislike anyone wearing a uniform, such as the postman. Some Maltipoos even notice skin color and react suspiciously. The only way to prevent your Maltipoo from reacting to people with unfamiliar features is to introduce it to all kinds of people while it is still a puppy.

Most puppies and dogs are wary around children; they don't see them as mini-humans but as strange creatures with loud voices, jerky movements and melodramatic emotions. Children scare and fascinate most dogs. The sad reality is that over 60 percent of dog bite victims are children. 75 percent of these dog bites are bites to the face. The only way to keep your dog from becoming part of that statistic is to socialize your dog with children from an early age.

It is very important to socialize your dog with children of all ages; just supervise closely any time they are together. Also, as your Maltipoo grows into an adult, it is important to continue socializing your dog with children, as it can quickly forget how to act around them.

How to do a meet and greet with someone new:

1. Carry some treats in your pocket to reward your dog after meeting someone new and acting properly. You can also give the new person some treats to share with your Maltipoo.
2. Ask the person to sit down; place your Maltipoo near them. Tell the person to just ignore your Maltipoo.
3. Let your Maltipoo make the first move--when it begins to smell the new person, the person can give it a biscuit and try to pet it.
4. Avoid sudden movements that might frighten your puppy.
5. Praise your puppy after it has made friends with the new person.
6. If your puppy remains skittish and uneasy, repeat the introduction another day until it is relaxed with the new person.

Let your Maltipoo become multicultural; let it meet as many people as possible. The more people it meets the better behaved it will become in social situations. Encourage polite children to pet your Maltipoo and maybe even give it a treat. Let it meet and greet people in wheelchairs, deliverymen, people with deep voices, nuns, even homeless people that are collecting bottles. The key is teaching it that there is nothing to be fearful of, that everyone is a friend and no one wants to hurt it or you.

Socializing with the postman

Why do most dogs just hate the mailman? It seems cliché, but it is true--dogs hate the mailman.

Well, it isn't just the mailman; it can be the pizza delivery guy, the UPS or FEDEX delivery person, basically anyone that approaches your front door is Public Enemy No.1. In your dog's eyes, they deserve to be barked at mercilessly.

How can you reduce this behavior? Let's begin with the reasons why your Maltipoo dislikes these people.

1. **Trespassing**: Maltipoos can become quite territorial and from your dog's point of view, these people are invaders and trespassing on its private property.
2. **The mailman comes back**: Your dog is pleased when the mailman appears to have listened to its warning barks and growls because he left. But imagine how your dog feels when the same guy comes back the very next day, and the day after, and the day after that! Your dog takes the daily visit from the postman as a personal insult.
3. **Chemical release**: Whenever your dog is provoked and angry, its brain releases several hormones or chemicals, which are addictive.

This chemical release is the reason for the repeated bad behavior to-wards to mailman.

4. **Habits become behavior**: If your dog's aggressive behavior to-wards the mailman isn't corrected, it becomes directed to anyone approaching the front door, and even any noises that it doesn't like, such as a vehicle horn honking. Allowing your dog to bark at the mail-man can lead to serious behavior issues later on in life that will be very difficult to correct.

How can you teach your Maltipoo to like the mailman?

Start early teaching your Maltipoo to accept the mailman, if possible right from the first day you bring it home. Put a treat in the mailbox and tell your mailman to come meet your new dog right away. This will teach your puppy that the mailman is a friend and it will be eager to welcome him to the house.

Another practical way to introduce your Maltipoo to the mailman is to do it on neutral ground. Before your mailman arrives at your house, have your Maltipoo on a leash and meet him a few houses away from yours. Your mailman can give it a treat and you both walk up to your house to-gether. Your Maltipoo won't even realize it is making friends with the mail-man until it's too late. You will need to repeat this process a few times.

By making sure it is familiar with the mailman, you can prevent your dog from barking at visitors as it gets older.

Six keys to having a well- balanced socialized dog:

The sooner you begin the socialization process the better. Continuing to introduce your dog to new people and animals throughout its whole life will help it act correctly around others.

These six suggestions can be applied to dogs of any age, it just might take longer to socialize an older dog that has issues with strangers. With patience and consistency, everything is possible.

1. Make it feel safe and secure: Fear leads to aggression and nervous-ness. When introducing your Maltipoo to a new situation or person, make sure your dog feels safe and secure. How can you do that? Let it meet the new person or animal on its own terms. Stand close to your dog, so it can hide between your legs if necessary. If meeting a person, ask them to give it a treat and talk in a low voice.

2. Teach your dog how to play without biting: If you allow your dog to bite you when playing, when it meets a new person or dog, it will as-sume that biting is an acceptable way of playing. It might accident-ly bite a bigger dog and get a bigger bite in return. Or it could bite a small child in the face and need to be euthanized.

3. Teach your dog to interact with other animals and all types of people: Make sure your Maltipoo gets to meet as many different people as possible: different races, tall and short, fat and skinny, with beards and canes or umbrellas. With animals, introduce it to cats, other dogs and anything that moves. Also, when it hears new noises, go and investigate with it, so it can see that these noises are no threat to either of you.

4. Teach your dog that you are the pack leader: The pack leader protects the pack and your Maltipoo will look to you for protection. If it is used to being in control and making its own decisions, it will assume the responsibility of being your pack leader. Then, when it is presented with a stranger or a new situation, it will freak out and begin to bark and act aggressively because it believes it needs to protect you.

5. Teach your dog to follow your lead: Your Maltipoo picks up on your attitude and reactions. When meeting a new person, reach out and shake hands; if it is an old friend, give them a hug, etc. Your dog will observe your behavior and most likely allow the person to pet it. When meeting other dogs, you can pet the dog to show your dog that it is friendly and nice. Do the same with other animals that you and your Maltipoo might meet. It will follow your lead.

6. Train your dog according to its age: Puppies can't handle more than three to four new tasks a day; adult dogs maybe four to five new tasks a day. Older dogs or rescued dogs can't handle more than two to three new tasks a day, maybe even less. If your dog didn't react well to a new situation, but was calm, be sure to praise it. This will build up its self-confidence.

Reminders when socializing your Maltipoo

Remember that socializing and obedience training are meant to be fun. If your dog is enjoying meeting new people and dogs or learning new commands, it will learn more quickly than if it is a burden or boring. Try to keep training fun.

If your Maltipoo is on the nervous or shy side, take your time. This isn't a race to teach your dog the fastest, you have to teach it at a speed that works and makes it feel comfortable.

Each year, thousands of dogs are euthanized for bad behavior that could have been avoided by taking the time to teach them when they were younger. Don't let your Maltipoo be one of the statistics.

Conclusion

" *Happiness is a warm puppy."*
Charles M. Schulz

Your Maltipoo has found the elixir to be an eternal puppy, thanks to its inherited genes from the Poodle and Maltese. Your Maltipoo will give you a lifetime of loyal companionship and joy.

Maltipoos are very intelligent dogs that are eager to please their owners, making them one of the easiest dogs to train. They make an ideal pet for first-time dog owners or elderly ones that lack the mobility for training a dog that is hyperactive or has a hardheaded temperament. Maltipoos are appreciated for their easygoing personality.

In these pages is everything you need to know about your Maltipoo puppy. It will help your Maltipoo grow into a happy, well-behaved and obedient dog. The suggestions provided in this book will help you train a puppy or even an adult Maltipoo that might have been rescued from an abusive home.

The only thing this book doesn't help you do is pick out the perfect name for your Maltipoo. We will leave that difficult task up to you!

The chapter on potty training your Maltipoo discusses various methods of how to potty train your puppy. If you follow the suggestions given, you should have successfully trained your Maltipoo in less than a week. If your Maltipoo is older, it will take a little longer than one week and more patience to potty train.

This book also provides practical advice on how to care for your Maltipoo's health and how to avoid future illnesses. Lots of details are given about how to groom your Maltipoo by yourself and how to brush its teeth.

As with everything in life, you get out of it what you put in to it. The more time and energy that you are willing to dedicate to training and bonding with your Maltipoo, the better-trained and more well-behaved dog you will have. Don't leave training up to the chance that it will become automatically trained; that isn't going to happen.

This book also discusses the importance of becoming your Maltipoo's pack leader. This will help it trust you and learn to have confidence in it-self. If it knows you are the dominant pack leader, it will not suffer from separation anxiety and will have better social skills with other people and animals.

As you learned, most of the long-term health problems your Maltipoo could have are because of bad breeder practices. Make sure to investi-gate the health history of your future Maltipoo's parents and make sure they have a clean bill of health. A little bit of research now could save you much heartache in the future.

We wish you and your Maltipoo a long and happy life together, and may this book become your manual to understanding and training your Maltipoo.

Happy Maltipoo, happy life!

Made in the USA
Monee, IL
16 September 2023

42869744R00090